PENGUIN BOOKS

T0051453

THE GETTING THINGS DONE WORKBOOK

DAVID ALLEN is an international bestselling author who is widely recognized as the world's leading expert on personal and organizational productivity. *Time* magazine called his flagship book, *Getting Things Done*, "the definitive business self-help book of the decade."

BRANDON HALL, PHD, coaches individuals and teams and speaks on high achievement and living with purpose. He wrote the first book about online learning for corporations decades ago and has presented at conferences around the world. He has been interviewed by *Fortune, Businessweek, Inc.,* and *Fast Company*. He has worked with IBM, Apple, GE, Kraft, Cisco, Exxon, 3M, Microsoft, and the Department of Defense.

THE

GETTING

DAVID ALLEN
and
BRANDON HALL

THINGS DONE
WORKBOOK

10 Moves to
Stress-Free Productivity

 PENGUIN BOOKS

PENGUIN BOOKS

An imprint of Penguin Random House LLC
penguinrandomhouse.com

LIBRARY OF CONGRESS CATALOGING-IN-PUBLICATION DATA

Names: Allen, David, 1945 December 28– author. | Hall, Brandon, 1951– author. |
Supplement to (work): Allen, David, 1945 December 28– Getting things done.
Title: The getting things done workbook : 10 moves to stress-free productivity / David Allen, Brandon Hall.
Description: New York, New York : Penguin Books, [2019]
Identifiers: LCCN 2019018372 (print) | LCCN 2019021832 (ebook) |
ISBN 9780525505228 (ebook) | ISBN 9780143133438 (paperback)
Subjects: LCSH: Time management—Problems, exercises, etc. |
Self-management (Psychology)—Problems, exercises, etc. |
Distraction (Psychology)—Problems, exercises, etc. |
BISAC: BUSINESS & ECONOMICS / Time Management. |
SELF-HELP / Time Management. | SELF-HELP / Stress Management.
Classification: LCC BF637.T5 (ebook) | LCC BF637.T5 A455 2019 (print) | DDC 158—dc23
LC record available at https://lccn.loc.gov/2019018372

Printed in the United States of America
3rd Printing

SET IN LINOLETTER
DESIGNED BY TANYA MAIBORODA

BRANDON HALL

For Brian, Karen, Steve, Kaylor, and future generations.
May you see projects, not problems, in your life and in the world.

To David and Kathryn, the most gracious and professional couple I have ever met.

DAVID ALLEN

For any and all of you who can't help but help yourselves improve
the quality of your lives and the world around you.

WHAT'S IN

Why You Need This!

HOW THIS WORKBOOK WORKS

x

THIS WORKBOOK

3

**The 10 Moves to
Stress-Free Productivity**

4

**More
GTD® Stuff**

5

**Your
Progress Tracker**

THE GETTING THINGS DONE WORKBOOK

1 WHY YOU

NEED THIS!

WE ALL NEED TO BE

Hi! I'm David, the guy who researched and wrote the *Getting Things Done* (GTD®) book so that you could enjoy a life of stress-free productivity.

Obviously, I believe you need to learn what it takes to be more productive with as little effort as possible, but **what really matters is what YOU think**. So let me ask you to take just a couple minutes to pick between "This" or "That" on this spread:

THIS
Calm under pressure
In control of your workload
In control of your time and life
Reliable place for ideas and tasks
Maintain perspective and trust in your focus
Get your email inbox to zero
Organized system for all paper

VS.

MORE PRODUCTIVE!

THAT
Overwhelmed and stressed
Little control and overloaded
Out of control of your time and life
Unreliable system and things fall through cracks
Go with the flow and hope for the best
Drown in email hell
Piles of papers and stuff

Okay, so I may be "leading the witness," as they say, but that is truly the reality. Every day you have a choice between this or that, and even when you have good intentions you may not know where to turn for proven principles and systems to help you get out from under the mountain of calls, emails, and paper.

That's where I come in! I have been studying human productivity since Adam . . . well, not quite. And I've seen how the digital revolution we are currently participating in has accelerated the universal issue of too much to do, too little time to do it.

WIIFM?

You may be asking, "What's in it for me?" If you make the choice to follow the steps and instructions in this Workbook and actually practice the ten moves . . . then you will most definitely and assuredly be the MOST . . .

PEACEFUL, ORGANIZED, HAPPY, EFFICIENT, RELIABLE, AND SUCCESSFUL HUMAN BEING EVER TO WALK THE EARTH!

Seriously! There is something amazing that happens when you free up your mind to do what it does best: think.

SO WHY NOT GIVE IT A TRY? WHAT DO YOU HAVE TO LOSE?

What If?

If you had more room in your head, what would you choose to be and do?

☐ **More creative?** What would you do?

_____

_____

☐ **More strategic?** What would you do?

_____

_____

☐ **More innovative?** What would you do?

_____

_____

☐ **More loving?** What would you do?

_____

_____

☐ **More present with whatever you're doing?** What would you do?

_____

_____

☐ **What else?**

_____

_____

_____

HOW THIS WORK

Working in this Workbook is as simple as 1, 2, 3, 4:

1. Review chapter 2, **"Start Here!,"** which follows . . . just so you get the big idea.

2. Start working on the ten moves . . . **IN YOUR OWN TIME**. But we recommend:

   - *Do the first three moves (about Capturing) as soon as possible.*

   - *Take your time with the rest of the moves—but ideally find one to two hours each week to complete a couple of them.*

   - *Go through the* **MOVES IN SEQUENCE**.

3. Keep track of your progress on the **LAST PAGE OF THIS WORKBOOK**. It feels good to make progress and to check things off.

4. Have fun! This stuff may initially seem mundane and potentially boring—but, believe me, there is a pot of gold at the end of this rainbow! And you will probably find it engaging to start to play within your own process, with your own stuff, in your real-time world, as we've laid it out for you. Many thousands of us do this regularly—join the club.

You are more creative than you probably know!

BOOK WORKS

Look for the following design markers throughout the Workbook to help you get to the next level of productivity prowess.

Insights Enjoy these stories and anecdotes from David Allen and the community of people who practice the GTD methodology (let's call them GTDers), including tips and tricks and words of wisdom and quotes from the author.

Deep Dive There will be principles you'll want to learn more about and in much more detail. We'll make sure to show you where you can go to learn more in this Workbook, in the GTD book itself, or in other locations via QR codes and web links.

FAQs Learn from the most frequently asked questions and answers courtesy of David and the GTD community.

Act Now! Whenever you see this icon know that this is your time and space in the Workbook to act on what you have learned! This is the time and place to write down any thoughts, ideas, and insights that will help you be more productive.

Progress Tracker As mentioned in #3, left, this is the place to track your own progress.

Checklists After you've completed the moves associated with each of the five GTD steps, you'll find a checklist that provides a quick summary of the moves that were covered. These checklists are the tools you can use moving forward that will assist you as you continue applying GTD in your life. Think of them as a summary cheat sheet of what you need to be doing.

"Be steady and well-ordered in your life so that you can be fierce and original in your work."

— GUSTAVE FLAUBERT

▶ START

2

HERE!

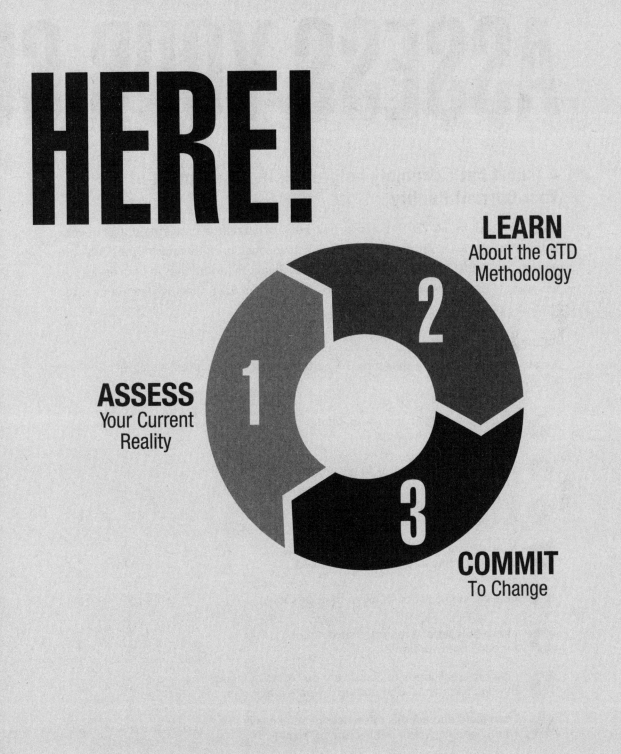

ASSESS
Your Current
Reality

LEARN
About the GTD
Methodology

COMMIT
To Change

ASSESS YOUR CU

!

A (short but extremely helpful) Self-Assessment of Your Current Reality

Before we dive into GTD, let's assess how you are currently managing things in your world. When you are rating the questions below, consider both your professional and your personal life. In both settings, you want to be more productive. In both areas, you will want to have perspective and control. Rate each of the following statements using the scale provided:

Rating Scale

1 = strongly disagree; **2** = disagree; **3** = neither agree nor disagree; **4** = agree; **5** = strongly agree

1	I write down ideas and to-do items when they first show up.	1	2	3	4	5
2	I keep a complete list of all my next actions.	1	2	3	4	5
3	I keep a record of what I am waiting for from other people.	1	2	3	4	5
4	My calendar contains only appointments or day-specific information that I need.	1	2	3	4	5
5	I have a single list of all my current projects.	1	2	3	4	5
6	I have at least one recorded next action for each of my projects.	1	2	3	4	5
7	I get my email inbox to zero every day or so by going through each email and putting it where it belongs.	1	2	3	4	5
8	I can store and access reference material easily when needed, whether it is paper or digital.	1	2	3	4	5

9	I have designated in-trays in all the places I need to capture all my incoming paper and stuff.	1 2 3 4 5
10	I get my paper in-tray(s) to empty every day or so.	1 2 3 4 5
11	When I get behind or overwhelmed, I know how to get back on track by engaging with my next actions, projects, and calendar.	1 2 3 4 5
12	I take time each week to get caught up and to review how I am doing with my professional/personal work.	1 2 3 4 5
13	I have a trusted place I can easily find and look at to see additional/support information about any project I am working on.	1 2 3 4 5
14	I have a framework I can use in order to best choose what to work on at any particular time.	1 2 3 4 5
15	When unexpected demands arise or interruptions occur, I can easily evaluate their priorities against everything else I have to do.	1 2 3 4 5

Total your score = _____ (out of 75)

Scoring Key

15–30: You really need this Workbook; don't worry, we will walk you through it.

31–46: You are getting a glimpse of what it feels like to live a productive life.

47–62: You are doing well! Keep going!

63–75: You are close to being masterful with GTD! This last fine-tuning will make a huge impact for you.

At the end of this Workbook, you will have the chance to reassess yourself in order to see your progress.

LEARN ABOUT

The GTD methodology for managing your workflow and achieving stress-free productivity consists of five steps. **This is important for you to understand, because the ten moves you are about to engage in all fall within these five steps.** Plus, it's always good to have the big-picture perspective before diving down into the details!

The 5 Steps of GTD

STEP 1 CAPTURE

STEP 2 CLARIFY

STEP 3 ORGANIZE

STEP 4 REFLECT

STEP 5 ENGAGE

FIVE STEPS

Scan and Learn More—The 5 Steps of GTD

go.gettingthingsdone.com/no-1

GTD

In order to understand GTD—and to appreciate its value for you—it is useful to understand workflow and the importance of having a system. And this must be an **external** system—not your head (which the brain scientists have concluded is a lousy office)!

Workflow

Workflow is the sequence of activities that takes inputs and commitments all the way from initiation to completion. It includes all the stuff that comes at you, from external sources and your own creative thinking, how you keep track of it, and what you do with it until it is done or discarded. It includes that request from your board of directors, that idea you have for your marketing campaign, your file about an upcoming project, and that email from your neighbor about trash pickup. This is what GTD helps you with—managing this flow of things that need your attention, personally as well as professionally.

System

You also need to have a system that is both complete and leakproof. More than anything, you need to have a system that you can trust. Imagine the reduction of stress you will have when you are confident that nothing is slipping through the cracks, when you have a comprehensive list of the activities and projects you need to take care of, and when you know where to locate the information that you need. You will find, as you implement each piece, step-by-step, that you can put your trust in it. Once you do that, you will rely on it like a faithful guide dog. You will learn to depend on it and will know that you can count on it, because you are attending to it and interacting with it nearly daily. As you do so, you will no longer need to keep track of things in your head, you will no longer need to remember to do this or that, and others will discover that they can count on you. Most important, you'll be able to count on yourself! Your confidence will increase, your stress will go down, and you will be on your way to being a master of GTD.

Step 1: Capturing

In this first step, you make sure to **Capture** all of your "incoming." This includes email, papers, notes from meetings, and commitments that come up in conversations and meetings. It also includes ideas you have, anything on your mind that you need to remember, and anything that has your attention. This means any coulds, shoulds, need-tos, might-want-tos, and ought-tos that weigh on your mind but that you haven't yet documented.

You will gather these items in a trusted place. It DOES NOT mean you do them right now; in this step, you simply *capture* them for later. In this Workbook, and as part of the ten moves, we'll discuss the ways you capture these items. The major ones include:

- Physical in-tray for paper
- Pen and paper
- Smartphone for making notes or voice reminders
- Email and texts

With GTD, you'll make these tools a part of your daily work style and lifestyle.

go.gettingthingsdone.com/no-2

Scan and learn more from David Allen about this step . . .

+

You can also find out more in chapter 5 of the GTD book.

Step 2: Clarifying

Once you have these things captured in one place, the next step is to **Clarify**, or process, each item to determine what needs to be done with it. You will learn best practices for Clarifying emails, voicemails, texts, and stacks of meeting notes that come your way.

In this step, you move your stuff from "In" to where it needs to be. You clarify what each item you have captured is, and you determine what next action to take regarding the item. Is it "trash"? Or is it "on hold for later review"?

WHY CLARIFYING IS SO IMPORTANT

You have all this paper and other items in your in-tray now. You have email coming in nonstop. Plus, you have all these ideas and next actions you have captured from your Mind Sweep (which we'll discuss later).

Without Clarifying, all the stuff you have captured remains in your "In." Without Clarifying, even though you have captured each item, your system will not be airtight. Without complete Clarifying, there is no hope for stress-free productivity. Your stuff remains only as "stuff."

You need to think about your stuff more than you think, but not as much as you're afraid you might.

—DAVID ALLEN

go.gettingthingsdone.com/no-3

Scan and learn more from David Allen about this step . . .

+

You can also find out more in chapter 6 of the GTD book.

Step 3: Organizing

Once you have clarified each item, you put the item either in the trash or into its proper place in your trusted system so that you can get to it when you need it. The **Organizing** step ensures that where something is matches up with where you can expect to find it. You will learn to organize actionable items you've identified with:

- A calendar that's up-to-date
- A list of your projects and your next actions
- A list of things you're waiting for
- Files for project plans and reference materials

> I'm not naturally organized (ask my wife!). I'm naturally lazy. I hate having to rethink what something is and what it means to me. That's why I put it in its place, so the thinking about it is done. Then I'm free to simply be making choices about which thing to engage with in the moment.
>
> **—DAVID ALLEN**

go.gettingthingsdone.com/no-4

Scan and learn more from David Allen about this step . . .

+

You can also find out more in chapter 7 of the GTD book.

Step 4: Reflecting

When you take the time to **Reflect** and get caught up, you stay on top of the things that you want and need to do something about. You will learn to review the big picture of your activities; you will have time to check in with yourself and to tweak your GTD system.

You'll learn how to make this reflecting time a part of your weekly schedule. This is a core component of the GTD methodology: the GTD Weekly Review®.

**Do something about what you're thinking,
and think about what you're doing.**

**Every so often we need to manage the forest
instead of simply hugging the trees.**

—DAVID ALLEN

go.gettingthingsdone.com/no-5

Scan and learn more from David Allen about this step . . .

+

Getting Things Done
the art of stress-free productivity
from the **New York Times** bestselling author
David Allen

An all-new updated edition ✓

You can also find out more in chapter 8 of the GTD book.

Step 5: Engaging

When you are *doing* your work, the **Engage** step involves taking the appropriate actions to complete your work with confidence. Choosing what to do in the moment—and trusting that your choice is the right one—makes up this final step of the GTD methodology.

You will see how to choose what to work on based on where you are and how much time and energy you have right now, as well as the multiple levels of your commitments with yourself and others.

Do. Or do not. There is no try.

—YODA

go.gettingthingsdone.com/no-6

Scan and learn more from David Allen about this step . . .

+

You can also find out more in chapter 9 of the GTD book.

COMMIT T

Where would you most like to be after completing this Workbook and implementing GTD? Imagine if there was nothing standing in the way of your getting what you want. Allow yourself to think big by imagining you couldn't fail. In the space below, list what you want for yourself.

1. What do you wish to accomplish in the next three to six months—at work and personally?
2. How do you want to be in terms of your stress level and confidence? How would you like to feel?
3. What are the two or three issues that you most want to resolve with improved productivity?
4. When the going gets tough, which it will, what will you say to yourself to keep going to the end of this Workbook and getting what you want from this work?
5. Who will you share your thoughts and commitments on this page with? (Change is easier when you are accountable to at least one other person.)

CHANGE

"They say that time changes things, but you actually have to change them yourself."

—ANDY WARHOL

THE
10 MOVES TO

3

STRESS-FREE PRODUCTIVITY

TRACK YOUR

There are ten moves or activities that make up the "doing" of GTD. When you have followed the step-by-step directions for these moves, you will have your GTD system in place. The reality is this: *you have a lot on your plate as is*. Seeing progress can keep you motivated, which is why we recommend keeping track of your progress in the last section in the Workbook.

GTD is made up of five steps. The following table shows us how the five steps are connected to the ten moves. Don't worry about memorizing this relationship at this time; it will be reinforced throughout the Workbook.

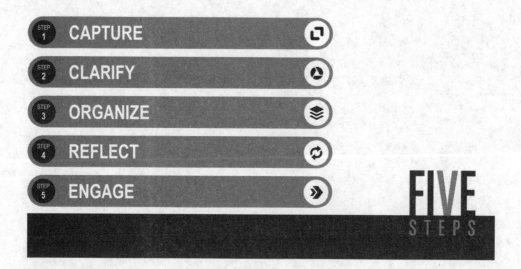

STEP 1 CAPTURE

STEP 2 CLARIFY

STEP 3 ORGANIZE

STEP 4 REFLECT

STEP 5 ENGAGE

FIVE STEPS

PROGRESS

THE 10 GTD MOVES

CAPTURE

Move 1	Capture All Your Incoming Paper into One In-tray	DATE
Move 2	Choose Your Capture Tool	DATE
Move 3	Do a Mind Sweep	DATE

CLARIFY

Move 4	Get Your In-tray to Empty	DATE
Move 5	Get Your Emails to Zero	DATE

ORGANIZE

Move 6	Create Your Next Actions and Other Lists	DATE
Move 7	Keep Track of Your Projects on One List	DATE
Move 8	Create Folders to Stay Organized	DATE

REFLECT & ENGAGE

Move 9	Do a GTD Weekly Review	DATE
Move 10	Conduct a Daily Review	DATE

"The way to get anything under control, whether it's your kitchen, your company, or your consciousness, is to capture, clarify, organize, reflect, and engage with it."

—DAVID ALLEN

Capture All Your Incoming Paper into One In-tray

Why You Need This Move!

IF your reality looks like this . . .

- Piles of papers, files, notes, stickies, and reminders lying around waiting to be handled, as soon as you "can get around to it"
- Not being able to find the notes from the phone call last week that include the info you need for today's meeting

IF you feel overwhelmed . . . and like things are out of control, and there is no clear way to get back in control without spending hours—or days—trying to get organized . . .

    IF this is you, then this move is the first step in getting to that organized place.

    It is the first step in setting up your GTD system which will help ensure that these issues get resolved and stay resolved, as far into the future as you maintain your use of GTD.

If you don't pay attention to what has your attention, it will take more of your attention than it deserves.

—DAVID ALLEN

Reality Check!

Take a couple of minutes to do a quick assessment of all the paper and other physical "stuff" in your life right now. Check all that apply:

What?	Number of Locations
☐ Piles of paper	
☐ Sticky notes	
☐ Reminders	
☐ Task lists	
☐ Notebooks with notes	
☐ Paper calendars	
☐ Other paper products you use	
☐ Miscellaneous things in or around your area that are not where or how they should be	

Step-by-Step

Step 1. Buy two in-trays to serve as your "In."

Step 2. Gather your loose papers, notes, and reminders and put them in your in-tray.

Step 1. Buy two in-trays to serve as your "In."

Keep one in-tray for work and one for home or personal use.

These in-trays will be your corrals where all of your incoming paper will reside temporarily. Your in-trays will hold these items until you're ready for the next steps (which we'll cover in future moves).

> Your *work in-tray* should be placed within arm's reach,
> usually on top of your desk.
>
> Your *home in-tray* should be in a location that is convenient
> to you and to others in your household, so they can
> place notes, mail, and other items there for you.

STOP HERE

Before you go further with the move, first buy your two in-trays, label them "In," and place them in the suggested locations.

Step 2. Gather your loose papers, notes, and reminders and put them in your in-tray.

- Gather all of your incoming mail, lists of things to do, reminders, sticky notes, and any other "stuff" that requires your attention. All of it.
- Put the items for WORK into your work in-tray.
- Put the items for personal or HOME into your home in-tray.

This move is key—it is the first essential part of your new GTD practice. The experience you will likely have when you make this move is an immediate sense of taking positive steps to get organized and in control of all that paper and stuff that is lying about and coming at you each day. Your in-tray should be the only landing spot for anything incoming.

WHAT NOW?

Where does all of the paper and stuff go from here? In a later move titled "Getting Your In-tray to Empty" you will learn best practices for what to do with these items. But don't go there yet! Instead continue in sequence with Move 2.

go.gettingthingsdone.com/no-7

Scan and learn more from David Allen about this move . . .

My wife, Kathryn, and I have had an in-tray for each of us in our home for decades, wherever we have lived. These days we happen to live in Amsterdam. Each in-tray is labeled with our name and is the designated place for mail, notes, or items we put there when the other is not available or we don't want to interrupt.

We can then enjoy each other's company, not distracted by all the "business of life" stuff that can encroach, because we each maintain a system to process it.

By the way, in Dutch in-trays are called *inbakjes*.

Congratulations!
You have successfully completed Move 1!

Go to the last page of the Workbook and update
Your Progress Tracker with today's date!

"Your mind is for *having* ideas, not for *holding* them."

—DAVID ALLEN

Choose Your Capture Tool

Why You Need This Move!

IF your reality looks like this . . .

- Have you ever left a meeting or conversation thinking you have an agreement, only to return to your desk and find that **nothing moves forward?** Neither by you nor others?

Usually, when nothing moves forward it's due to the fact that no one captured the *item that needs action*. Next actions are fundamental to making progress in your life. Capturing—and keeping track of—your actionable items is critical to your success.

In a later move, you'll create a Next Actions list. Without capturing things that need action, stuff doesn't get remembered and doesn't happen. In short, things slip through the cracks. Capturing these things seals those cracks.

This move, capturing actionable items by writing them down, is a powerful driving force to use to keep yourself and others moving forward productively. This simple practice not only will improve your ability to complete things, it will encourage an action focus in those around you.

WHAT OTHERS HAVE SAID . . .

"I've been capturing next actions now for years. I could not begin to tell you the number of times that I've used it, with whomever I'm working—team members, customers, suppliers, family. While they will make a 'mental note,' I pull out my notebook and write it down. They know that I'm taking what they say seriously and they respect that."

"The small notepad I keep at hand is brilliant! I use it constantly. It goes everywhere with me. . . ."

"I dictate an email to myself anytime, anywhere—it has changed my habits."

Step-by-Step

Step 1. Always have a capture tool at hand.

Step 2. Capture each actionable item or idea as it occurs, especially in meetings, conversations, and personal reflections.

Step 3. At least once a day, collect your captured notes and put them in your in-tray.

Step 1. Always have a capture tool at hand.

This could be either a smartphone or pen and paper.

SMARTPHONE

Perhaps you prefer to use your smartphone, since for most people it is always nearby. You could:

- Use a note-taking app to write
- Or a recording app to dictate
- Or send yourself an email.

PEN AND PAPER

If you prefer pen and paper, always have a small pad and pen in your pocket or purse.

David says: "Ninety-five percent of my capture is done low-tech—with pen and paper. It eliminates my resistance to capturing. No clicks, batteries, or Wi-Fi required!"

Reality Check!

What is your preference? We all have one. Take a moment to be honest with yourself, and find out which capture tool you naturally gravitate toward. Don't default to the tool you think you'd like to use, just because it's cool or handy.

1. There is no one right answer—just what's right for you—so are you a digital or paper user?
2. How do you currently and naturally capture things? Digital note, written note, email, audio recording?
3. If you were to choose the ideal way to capture next actions, how would you like to do it?

Step 2. Capture each actionable item or idea as it occurs, especially in meetings, conversations, and personal reflections.

Don't let any more good ideas or agreed-upon actions slip through the cracks.

Here are some examples of how GTDers capture next actions and ideas as they occur:

"I write things on cards I carry in my purse."

"I send myself emails from my smartphone."

"I jot things in my small notepad I carry in my pocket."

"I keep a pen and notepad on each of my desks, to jot anything down that shows up."

Step 3. At least once a day, collect your captured notes and put them in your in-tray.

You have notes from meetings, odd notes you have made, and ideas you have written down. Grab all of these and put them into your "In."

Alternatively, throughout the day, you can write them directly to the appropriate list (digital or paper), such as Next Actions, Waiting For, Someday/Maybe, or other. (You will set up these and other lists later.)

That's it. Simple—and Huge.

Frequently Asked Questions

Choose Your Capture Tool

What if my partner or my team does not practice GTD? Can I still capture next actions in front of them?

Yes. You can help focus and influence the productivity and actions of others around you with this simple practice. For teams whose members are GTD practitioners, this becomes the norm. But even if you are the lone GTDer, you can influence the culture when you're working in this way.

Do I need capturing tools for both my home and office?

Yes. They will likely be the same. You want something handy and reliable wherever you are.

Is one capture tool better than another?

Not necessarily. The best capturing tool is one that is easy and fast for you to use. Whiteboards are erased, sticky notes are misplaced, and neither is as effective as a notepad or a smartphone.

How many capture tools should I have?

Fewer tools is better. While a smartphone can always be with you, a larger pad is good for taking notes in meetings or on phone calls.

Be sure to move these captured items into your in-tray daily, or onto one of your lists.

You increase your productivity and creativity exponentially when you make it a habit to capture the right things at the right time. Capturing potentially actionable items as they occur to you will help you get things out of your head and onto paper or into a digital device. Doing this will help you accomplish more both at work and at home.

Congratulations!
You have successfully completed Move 2!

Go to the last page of the Workbook and update
Your Progress Tracker with today's date!

"Your head is a crappy office."

—DAVID ALLEN

MOVE 3

Do a Mind Sweep

Why You Need This Move!

In **Move 1** you CAPTURED all your incoming paper and stuff in one place.

In **Move 2** you identified how you CAPTURE all ideas and next actions that flow to you throughout the day.

In **Move 3** you'll CAPTURE all of the things you have on your mind and put them down on paper. Your mind is for *having* ideas, not *holding* them. Doing a Mind Sweep allows you to get things out of your head and into your GTD system.

If you are like most people, you have a lot on your mind: things that need to be captured and written down. The truth is, you should be writing down anything that has your attention, including:

- Things you have committed to doing
- Things you want to do
- Things you are thinking about doing
- Creative ideas that you don't want to slip away

When you write these down, you get them out of your head and onto paper, and into your "In." You are also likely to find that doing a Mind Sweep simply makes you *feel better*. Your mind is free and clear. There is no longer anything that you are trying to remember to do or that you're worried you might forget.

Mind Like Water®

Imagine having a completely clear mental space, with nothing unproductive pulling or pushing on you. You could dedicate 100 percent of your attention to whatever was at hand, with no distractions. You would be present. You would be mindful. The control of your attention would be available to you, without distraction.

"Mind Like Water" is the experience of being in which your mind is clear and you are capable of freely focusing on what you want. You are ready for anything. The GTD methodology overall is designed to get you there, and especially in this move: empty your mind with a Mind Sweep regularly.

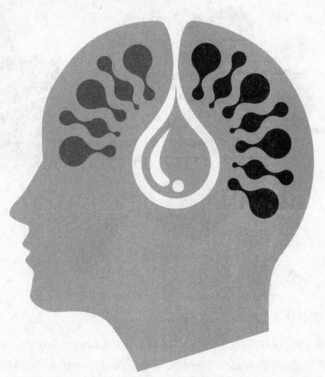

Step-by-Step

Step 1. Schedule twenty to thirty minutes for a Mind Sweep.

Step 2. Complete your first Mind Sweep.

Step 3. Place what you have captured in your in-tray.

Step 1. Schedule twenty to thirty minutes for a Mind Sweep.

WHAT IS A MIND SWEEP ANYWAY?

A Mind Sweep is simply writing down all that is on your mind. It's a way to completely clear your mind by capturing whatever is on your mind and putting it down on paper.

Step 2. Complete your first Mind Sweep.

1. Find a quiet place, if at all possible, where you can work on this move.
2. Have a pen and a stack of paper at hand. You can also use the next few blank pages in this Workbook if you'd prefer.
3. Start capturing *each* thought or idea or project that is on your mind and has your attention. Think of this as a *complete* brain dump.
4. Putting each thought on a separate piece of paper will make the next moves easier; but writing them in a long list or even recording yourself on a digital device can also work, if you choose.

Mind Sweep

Mind Sweep

Mind Sweep

Mind Sweep

Step 3: Place what you have captured in your in-tray.

Put all your pieces of paper, any lists you've made, and any other miscellaneous articles into your in-tray.

The coolest thing about a well-functioning in-tray is that it means you don't need to think or decide about stuff until you're ready to do that, and you don't miss anything that might be valuable to think and decide about at a later time.

WHAT NOW?

Where do all of these things go from here? In the later move titled "Get Your In-tray to Empty" you will learn best practices for what to do with these and all other items in your in-tray.

Grief and Relief!

It is common to experience both *grief* and *relief* after doing a Mind Sweep.

Grief can stem from items coming forward that had been tucked away in your mind for too long. This might include things you had promised yourself or someone else you would do. Now these items are in your system, and you can decide what to do about them.

Relief comes from getting all these items out of your head and into your system. Getting a grip on your current realities, for better or worse, is always a positively productive starting place.

Future Mind Sweeps

For Mind Sweeps that you do in the future, use the following Incompletion Trigger Lists—personal and professional—to spark more things to capture.

Mind Sweep Incompletion Trigger List: PERSONAL List

What has your attention?

PERSONAL

PROJECTS started, not completed

PROJECTS that need to be started

PROJECTS I have with other organizations

"LOOK INTO" projects

COMMITMENTS/PROMISES TO OTHERS

COMMUNICATIONS TO MAKE/GET

UPCOMING EVENTS

ADMINISTRATION

LEISURE

FINANCIAL

PETS

LEGAL

WAITING FOR

FAMILY

HOME/HOUSEHOLD

HEALTH

PERSONAL DEVELOPMENT

TRANSPORTATION

CLOTHES

ERRANDS

COMMUNITY

Future Mind Sweeps

Mind Sweep Trigger Incompletion List: PROFESSIONAL List

What has your attention?

PROFESSIONAL

PROJECTS started, not completed
PROJECTS that need to be started
"LOOK INTO" projects
COMMITMENTS/PROMISES TO OTHERS
COMMUNICATIONS TO MAKE/GET
WRITING TO FINISH/SUBMIT
READ/REVIEW
FINANCIAL
PLANNING/ORGANIZING
ORGANIZATION DEVELOPMENT
MARKETING/PROMOTION
ADMINISTRATION
STAFF/PARTNERS
SYSTEMS
SALES
MEETINGS
WAITING FOR
PROFESSIONAL DEVELOPMENT
WARDROBE

Frequently Asked Questions

Do a Mind Sweep

How long does it usually take to do a Mind Sweep?

It might take twenty minutes to an hour—or longer—to clear your mind and write down each item. It takes longer the first few times—you will likely have a lot to "download." Once you are doing Mind Sweeps regularly, you may find they take less time. On the other hand, you may find this is a useful, creative process for you, and it is worth any added time.

What's the best place and time of day to do a Mind Sweep?

You can do a Mind Sweep whenever and wherever you can set aside time and have paper handy. Experienced GTDers will do a short Mind Sweep whenever they have a few extra minutes—while waiting for the dentist, traveling on an airplane, etc.

Are you a nature-oriented type? You can always do an outdoor Mind Sweep! In fact, being in nature can sometimes help facilitate a relaxed mind, perfect for a Mind Sweep.

If I come up with something that I could complete quickly, right away, can I go ahead and do it?

Sure. But the benefit of this process is allowing yourself the luxury of emptying your mind, without letting it get distracted into your "doing." Best practice is to make this move as a separate step. Once you complete your Mind Sweep, take whatever action you choose. It will undoubtedly be a better choice.

Doing a Mind Sweep regularly makes you feel better by clearing your mind. Remember, your mind is for *having* ideas, not *holding* them. Get those ideas out of your head and onto paper, and you'll feel more mentally balanced, with less stress.

You increase your productivity and creativity exponentially when you make it a habit to capture potentially meaningful things in the moment they occur.

Congratulations!
You have successfully completed Move 3!

Go to the last page of the Workbook and update
Your Progress Tracker with today's date!

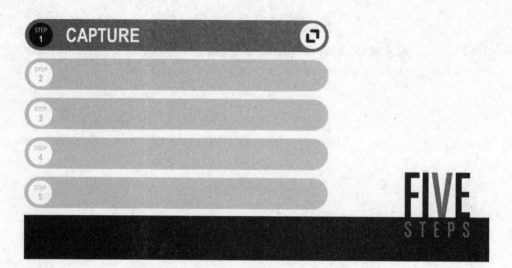

STEP 1 CAPTURE

STEP 2

STEP 3

STEP 4

STEP 5

FIVE STEPS

Your Checklist for the Capturing Moves

Move 1: Capture All Your Incoming Paper into One In-tray

- ☐ I have an in-tray in my work location.
- ☐ I have an in-tray for home or personal use.
- ☐ At least once daily, I gather any lists, notes, and voicemails to return and place them into my in-tray.
- ☐ If an item is too big to go into my in-tray, I have written a note that describes it and have placed it in the in-tray.

Move 2: Choose Your Capture Tool

- ☐ I have a capture tool, such as a smartphone or pen and paper, always at hand.
- ☐ I capture each next action or idea as it occurs, especially in meetings and conversations.

Move 3: Do a Mind Sweep

- ☐ I have completed my first Mind Sweep and written down everything that's on my mind, both work related and personal.
- ☐ I wrote each idea on a separate piece of paper, on a list, or in a separate section in this Workbook, and placed them into my in-tray to be Clarified at a later time.
- ☐ I have scheduled a regular time to do a Mind Sweep.

"A commitment kept only in your head will be given too much or too little attention."

—DAVID ALLEN

Get Your In-tray to Empty

Why You Need This Move!

You now have all your paper and other items sitting in your in-trays and you've captured your next actions. Now you need to move them out of your "In" by determining what to do with each item, so that . . .

- You will be more on top of your work, with less stress and more productivity.
- You will know that nothing important is being missed.
- Your stress will be lower.
- You will **feel** more in control—and you will **be** more in control—of your work and life.

This is a *crucial* step, and one that requires a specific GTD decision-making process that we'll walk you through.

Getting your in-tray to empty *doesn't mean* that all your work is done. It just means that you've made decisions about what to do with all the items in your in-tray and you have placed them where they should go. This move requires that you also have other parts of your GTD system in place, which we will set up in the next GTD step, **Organizing.** You will see mention here of a Waiting For category, Next Actions category, Someday/Maybe category, and Reference category. Hang tight, we will get to those.

Why Your In-tray Is Full

If you have been going through the moves in sequence, your in-tray is most likely piled high with *stuff* that needs your attention. This is neither bad nor wrong, but it will get in the way of stress-free productivity if it stays there too long. An in-tray can get full, and remain that way, for the following three reasons:

1. You have lots of incoming, and you know this is the place to corral it. Good for you!

2. You have no system set up to empty it. If you do not have a system for storing and keeping track of important items, your in-tray becomes the holding place—which is very inefficient. In the move that follows, you will set up a complete filing system and lists. (We recognize the chicken-and-egg problem here: learning the GTD steps in sequence or going out of sequence. Bear with us; we will cover that next.)

3. You don't trust your system. If you have your lists and files set up but you are not using them, perhaps you don't trust your system. Once you use them consistently, you build trust in your system, and there is no bottleneck to your flow of stuff coming in.

A "trusted system" means not only that you trust the contents of your "external brain" but that you will engage with the appropriate parts at the appropriate times.

—DAVID ALLEN

The Two-Minute Rule

By now it is obvious that you need to go through and Clarify all of the items in your "In." Here is where you should understand and implement the "two-minute rule," which is a method for quickly moving things forward and reducing items on your plate. It is a simple and direct way to increase your productivity.

What Is the Two-Minute Rule?

If a next action can be done in two minutes or less, do it now. That's it!

Why Two Minutes?

Two minutes is more or less the point where it starts to take longer to store and track a next action than to deal with it the first time you have it in your hands or see it in your email inbox. It's the efficiency cutoff. It can be applied independently of any other move, and its benefits occur right away.

Responding to Email

In many cases, responding to an email takes only a minute or two. If you find that you end up spending more time in your inbox than you had planned, given other commitments, simply delay processing your inbox until a later time (perhaps doing an interim "emergency scan" so you can relax about the delay; this is covered later, in Move 10).

Responding to Voicemail

Responding to a voicemail will often take less than two minutes—if you reach the caller's voicemail. If the call recipient picks up, that conversation can last quite a bit longer than two minutes. Some people respond to a voicemail with an email—to ensure that it is handled quickly. Alternatively, there are apps available that allow you to leave a message directly on someone's mobile phone, without the phone ringing.

More on the Two-Minute Rule

Does it have to be two minutes?

Two minutes is the general guideline—the cutoff where it makes sense to do it now, rather than defer it. Like the other moves of GTD, once you understand the best practice, you choose how to use it in your world.

What if I have a hundred two-minute actions?

Once you implement the GTD methodology, you are unlikely to have a backlog of two-minute actions. You will only need to take care of the new ones that show up in your email and your in-tray. To get past the backlog, you may need to gather them, put them in a folder, and write a next action to clarify them, or schedule time to do them in chunks of dedicated time.

What do I do when I complete a two-minute action?

Nothing! There's nothing you need to track. You just get the two-minute action done.

If your two-minute action results in another action—like refilling printer toner, only to discover you're out of toner entirely—then you'll need to take the appropriate steps to do, delegate, or defer the newly created action accordingly.

"Clarifying, getting your "In" to empty, doesn't mean actually *doing* all those things. It just means identifying each item and deciding what it is and where it goes."

—DAVID ALLEN

Step-by-Step

Getting your in-tray to empty requires the following actions, and in this order. (Analog Version)

Step 1. Pick up the top item in your in-tray. Ask, "What is it?"

Step 2. Ask, "Is it actionable?"

Step 3. If the answer to whether it is actionable is "NO, it is NOT actionable," ask "What to do with it?"

- *Trash it*
- *Store as reference material*
- *Incubate it (put it in your Someday/Maybe list location)*

Step 4. If the answer to whether it is actionable is "YES, it IS actionable," ask, "What's the next action?"

- *Do now, if less than two minutes*
- *Delegate to someone else (put it in your Waiting For folder)*
- *Defer to do yourself later (put it in your Next Actions folder; if you need to take the action by a specific date, add it to your calendar)*

Step 5. If there are more steps to do on this than the first one, what's the project title?

Whew! Those are the actions for Clarifying. You will notice they are precise. That precision is what ensures that nothing ever again slips through the cracks.

This move is crucial for mastering your workflow. Some people find it challenging because it requires a decision for each item. With practice, it will become second nature to you and you will become master of your incoming.

go.gettingthingsdone.com/no-8

Watch David explain the Clarify process.

Step-by-Step

Getting your in-tray to empty requires the following actions, and in this order. (Graphical Version)

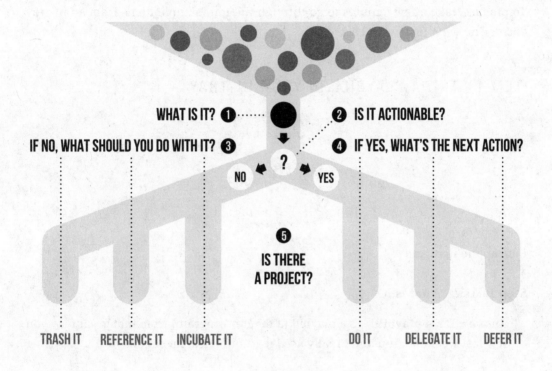

WHAT IS IT? ❶ ······

❷ IS IT ACTIONABLE?

IF NO, WHAT SHOULD YOU DO WITH IT? ❸

❹ IF YES, WHAT'S THE NEXT ACTION?

NO   ?   YES

❺
IS THERE
A PROJECT?

TRASH IT   REFERENCE IT   INCUBATE IT

DO IT   DELEGATE IT   DEFER IT

Empty Your In-tray Simulation

To practice, take a few minutes to go through the four sample items from an in-tray and decide what to do with each one.

ITEM 1 OF 4: A PLAYBILL IN YOUR IN-TRAY

Pick up the item and . . .

Step 1. Ask, "What is it?"

Answer: **It's a playbill!** It's a playbill (a theater program) from that great play you saw last weekend. You don't really *need* it . . . but it is a nice memento.

Step 2. Is it actionable? *(Check one)*

☐ Yes
☐ No

Answer: No. This item doesn't seem to be actionable.

Step 3. What do you do with it? *(Check one)*

☐ Trash it
☐ Store as reference material
☐ Incubate it in your Someday/Maybe folder

Your Answer

Trash it. From your earlier reaction to it, it seems you liked the idea of keeping it as a memento. So what else could you do with it? Choose another option.

Store as reference material. This seems the right option. While it is not strictly reference info, this is the broad category that includes keepsake items. Create and use a "Keepsakes" folder.

Incubate it in your Someday/Maybe folder. From your earlier reaction to it, it seems you saw it as not actionable, so no need to put it in your Someday/Maybe folder.

ITEM 2 OF 4: AN INVITATION IN YOUR IN-TRAY

Pick up the item and . . .

Step 1. Ask, "What is it?"

>*Answer:* **It's a wedding invitation.** Aziz and Tina are getting married! Aziz and Tina's big event will take place later in the year and on the other side of the country. You want to go.

Step 2. Is it actionable? *(Check one)*

☐ Yes
☐ No

>*Answer:* Yes, this item is indeed actionable—even if you did not want to go.

(Skip step 3 since it is actionable.)

Step 4. What's the next action? *(Check one and then read feedback for each answer below)*

☐ Discuss travel plans with your family.
☐ Mail the RSVP.
☐ Create a Project folder and label it "Attend Aziz and Tina's Wedding."

Your Answer

Discuss travel plans with your family. Remember, a next action finishes something or moves it forward. Although you might need to discuss travel with your family later, is there a better next action? (Hint: Will this require multiple steps?) Try again.

Mail the RSVP. Consider the other options. Remember, a next action finishes something or moves it forward. Is there a better next action? (Hint: Will this require multiple steps?) Try again.

Create a Project folder and label it "Attend Aziz and Tina's Wedding." Yes. There you go! There are multiple actions required. In this folder, you can add the invitation, your plan, the wedding registry, receipts, travel itineraries, and so on to keep everything in one place. (There are a couple of other steps also—see next part.)

So your next action is to create a Project folder.

Step 4 *(continued)*. **Do it now? Will it take less than two minutes?** *(Check one)*

☐ Yes
☐ No

Your Answer

If you answered Yes. With your blank folders labeler at arm's reach, you can create the Project folder in less than two minutes.

If you answered No. You're right! You will need to create a folder and label it. But there's something else you need to do to process this item. Let's see what that is.

Step 4 *(continued)*. **Delegate or defer?** You've created a Project folder for Aziz and Tina's wedding. Before adding the invitation to the folder, check the deadline for the RSVP. What do you need to do with that date? *(Check one)*

☐ Delegate it
☐ Defer it—put it on your Next Actions list
☐ Defer it—put it on your calendar

Your Answer

Delegate it. You could have an assistant take note of the RSVP deadline date, but isn't it more efficient to do it yourself? Choose another option.

Defer it—put it on your Next Actions list. You could add this to your Next Actions list as a reminder, but is there a better way to handle it? Consider another option.

Defer it—put it on your calendar. Yes. Before you stash the RSVP card into your "Aziz and Tina's Wedding" folder, put the deadline date into your calendar. (You will also want to add it to your Projects list, and write a next action, such as "Draft ideas about attending wedding.")

ITEM 3 OF 4: A REMINDER NOTE IN YOUR IN-TRAY

Pick up the item and . . .

Step 1. Ask, "What is it?"

> *Answer:* **It's a reminder note.** You wrote this note to remind yourself to return your optometrist's call to confirm Wednesday's appointment. (It would have been more efficient to write this directly into your calendar. However, on occasion, we only have time to make a quick note.)

Step 2. Is it actionable? *(Check one)*

☐ Yes
☐ No

Your Answer

If you answered Yes. Yes, confirming the appointment is the action to take.

If you answered No. This item is actionable. After all, it was a reminder for you to take some action.

(Skip step 3 since it is actionable.)

Step 4. What's the next action? *(Check one)*

☐ Get with the optometrist's office
☐ Call the optometrist's office
☐ Optometrist office

Your Answer

If you answered Get with the optometrist's office. "Get with" is vague. (See the list of next action verbs on page 121). Try another option.

If you answered Call the optometrist's office. That's right! This is a perfectly worded next action as it defines a specific, tangible action and starts with a concise action verb.

If you answered Optometrist's office. We added this one because people often make such a very brief, vague note to remind themselves. That is not a best practice. Instead, state your next action as a specific, tangible action item that begins with a concise action verb.

Step 4 *(continued).* Do it now? Will it take less than two minutes? *(Check one)*

☐ Yes
☐ No

Your Answer

If you answered Yes. A confirmation call will likely take just a minute or two, so you can *do it now* rather than put it off.

If you answered No. Actually, a quick confirmation call will likely take just a minute or two, so you can *do it now* rather than put it off.

Pick up the item and . . .

Step 1. Ask, "What is it?"

Answer: **It's your draft of the project report, with comments.** This is a hard copy of your report, with comments from your colleague. You know you will need to consolidate the notes and revise the report before you send it to the group manager.

Step 2. Is it actionable? *(Check one)*

☐ Yes
☐ No

Your Answer

If you answered Yes. Yes, there is work to be done.

If you answered No. Actually, this item is actionable. You have to compile the notes.

(Skip step 3 since it is actionable.)

Step 4. What's the next action? *(Check one)*

☐ Revise the project report.
☐ Take time now to read the report and the comments.
☐ Put the report back in the in-tray.

Your Answer

If you answered Revise the project report. Right! The wording for this next action is concise and uses a specific action verb.

If you answered Take time now to read the report and the comments. When we come across something interesting in our in-tray, it is tempting to drop what we are doing (Clarifying our in-tray to empty) to spend time on it. It is always your choice, of course. However, staying focused on the task at hand, especially getting your "In" to empty, will contribute to greater productivity with less stress. It's a best practice.

If you answered Put the report back in the in-tray. Of course not—although we are all tempted sometimes! When you sense that your energy is low, instead of picking up the next item in your in-tray, take a break, or do something that gets you moving.

Step 4 *(continued)*. **Do it now? Will it take less than two minutes?** *(Check one)*

☐ Yes
☐ No

Your Answer

If you answered Yes. Choose the other answer. It will take more than two minutes to revise the report.

If you answered No. Correct. Revising the report will take more than two minutes.

Step 4 *(continued)*. **Delegate or defer?** *(Check one)*

☐ Delegate it.
☐ Defer it—put it on your Next Actions list.
☐ Defer it—put it on your calendar.

Your Answer

Delegate it. If you can delegate it, then good. However, nothing in this example suggests that is an option. Assume you need to do the writing. Make another choice.

Defer it—put it on your Next Actions list. Yes, put it on your Next Actions list. You could also put it on your calendar if there is a due date. If you have a Project folder for this report, put the report in it. If you don't, make one.

Defer it—put it on your calendar. Yes, you can put it on your calendar, if there is a due date, or if you want to schedule time to work on it. If not, you could put it on your Next Actions list.

INSIGHTS

Remember, when you pick up something from your in-tray or open an email, never put it back into "In." It's a bad habit to remove an item from "In" and then not make a decision about what it means or what you're going to do with it and leave it in your in-tray.

Deciding to "not decide" about any item in your in-tray drains your psychological fuel tank and causes you to work less efficiently. Like any new habit, getting your in-tray to empty is a skill that will take time and effort to master using GTD. It may feel uncomfortable, just like other new practices felt uncomfortable at first. Remember learning how to drive a car? Remember your first semester at college? Remember when you were a first-time supervisor? You are the one to choose when to get your in-tray to empty. You don't have to do it all at once. You may want to hit it several times a day to keep it at empty.

"Emergency scanning" the contents of your in-tray first thing each morning and occasionally during the day to see if there are any fires that need to be put out is often necessary. But that works only if you return to your in-tray and clarify all your email regularly.

Now It's Your Turn

Turn to your in-tray and spend a few minutes practicing the Clarifying process you have just learned.

STOP HERE

Before you go to the next move, first make sure you are familiar and comfortable with the Clarify process.

If you still have concerns or questions we recommend . . .

go.gettingthingsdone.com/no-9

Scan and learn more from David Allen about this step.

+

You can also find out more in chapter 6 of the GTD book.

Frequently Asked Questions

Get Your In-tray to Empty

This process takes too much time. I don't have enough time as it is!

It does take time, especially at first. But what is the alternative? If items come into your in-tray, you have to get them out—often the sooner, the better. You can reduce your incoming: if mail is the problem, get off mailing lists. For the items you are placing in your in-tray, try putting less in by placing them where they go directly. You do this when you are bringing in groceries. You don't put your groceries in a holding area; you put them where they go directly—the pantry, the fridge, and so on. If you find you have a lot of written reminders for yourself in your in-tray, put them directly on your Next Actions list, Projects list, or calendar.

Consider whether handling this incoming is, in fact, part of your job. You may need to reframe it: this is part of your work, not busywork that is in the way of doing your "real" work.

What if an item requires that I make some big decision about something?

If you need more information or time to consider it, make it a project with a next action. Then you can prepare what's needed—even if you need to gather internal strength to make a tough decision. The important point is to remember the specific purpose of this move: to get items out of your in-tray to where they belong.

What happens if I'm processing an item and I don't have a folder for it?

You can add as many A–Z physical folders as you need and decide how you want to store digital information by topic. Simply grab a folder and your label maker and make the new folder, and/or make a digital storage folder in your computer. Then place the item in the appropriate spot in your file drawer or computer. If your drawer becomes more than three-quarters full, start a new drawer or purge what you have. We will cover this more in Organizing.

We've suggested this already, but it can't be emphasized enough: Getting "In" to empty doesn't mean actually doing all the things indicated on every note, reminder, etc. It just means identifying each item and deciding where it goes.

Congratulations!
You have successfully completed Move 4!

Go to the last page of the Workbook and update
Your Progress Tracker with today's date!

"The quicker my responses, the more people actually think before they send me stuff."

—DAVID ALLEN

Get Your Email to Zero

Why You Need This Move!

If you believe that having hundreds of emails in your inbox is normal and you are okay with it, you may be asking yourself, "Why do I need this move?" Take a look at the following "THIS vs. THAT" alternatives and then decide for yourself what you should do:

THIS—No, it is not worth it BECAUSE . . .

This move sounds too hard or complicated.

This will take too much time each day.

I am too busy to learn this.

I have bigger fish to fry than worrying about email.

I have gotten along so far doing it my way.

Email is not solvable, no matter what you do.

Maybe I will just scan this move and see if I like it.

THAT—Yes, it is worth it BECAUSE . . .

I want to move things forward and be more productive, with less stress.

Having items in my email inbox will distract me and nag at me every time I look at it, regardless of how much I say "It doesn't matter" to myself.

I want to feel more confident and in charge of my work and life.

I want to be in control of my work and life, and I want to get out from behind the eight ball.

This is the do-the-laundry, brush-my-teeth part of using email, with similar consequences for skipping it.

If you choose to continue with this move, which we highly recommend, you will know that every email has been taken care of. You will learn to do it briskly, in a way that gives you power and confidence. There will be no embarrassing time bombs that you missed. Ultimately, this move is about taking control of your email. It is a simple prescription: Get your email inbox to zero every day or so by clarifying each email message and putting it where it needs to be—including the trash.

When you get your inbox to zero, your productivity will be up, your stress will be down, and your sense of control may well be through the roof! That is a wonderful feeling. You may also feel exceptional, because you will be. You will be one of the few who uses a daily practice to tame the email monster. You also might find yourself doing what lots of GTDers do, especially the first few times. You might find yourself proclaiming, out loud, to no one in particular, "Email to zero!"

Step-by-Step

Getting your email inbox to zero follows the same process you just learned in Move 4 for your physical in-tray. (Analog Version)

Step 1. For each email in your inbox, look at it and ask, **"What is it?"**

Step 2. Then ask, **"Is it actionable?"**

Step 3. If the answer to whether it is actionable or not is "**NO, it is NOT actionable**," either

- *Delete it*
- *Incubate it (put it in your Someday/Maybe list or folder), or*
- *Store it (put it in a Reference folder)*

Step 4. If the answer to whether it is actionable or not is "**YES, it IS actionable**," ask, **"What's the next action?"**

- *Do it now (Remember the two-minute rule?)*
- *Delegate it (once you've done that, place it in your Waiting For folder)*
- *Defer it (place it in your Next Actions folder; if you need to take the action by a specific date, add it to your calendar)*

Step 5. If there are more steps to do, what's the project title?

To be clear, this does not mean that you have to *do* every task related to those emails—only that each email has been reviewed and put in its proper place.

MOVE 5
Step-by-Step

Getting your email inbox to zero follows the same process you just learned in the previous move. (Graphical Version)

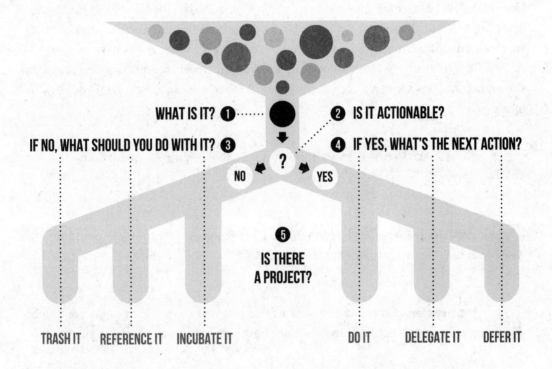

WHAT IS IT? **1**

2 IS IT ACTIONABLE?

IF NO, WHAT SHOULD YOU DO WITH IT? **3**

4 IF YES, WHAT'S THE NEXT ACTION?

?

NO

YES

5
IS THERE
A PROJECT?

TRASH IT   REFERENCE IT   INCUBATE IT

DO IT   DELEGATE IT   DEFER IT

You have permission to make a photocopy of this page so that you can post it in your work area as you learn this model.

Create New Folders

In order to get your email inbox to zero, you will need to create some new email folders. (Yes, technically, setting up new folders is part of the Organizing step of GTD. However, the folders need to be in place in order to get those emails to zero now.)

Start by creating the four folders in your email program and labeling them as shown below. These folders are where you will move emails as you go through your inbox.

 Next Actions—This will hold emails that require a next action on your part.

 Waiting For—Here is where you will keep emails that are reminders of action you are waiting for from someone.

 Someday/Maybe—Here is where you will keep action items you might want to take in the future—but not now.

Reference—This is where you will store emails you want to keep for possible reference later, but that do not require action. (If you're already using email reference folders, just continue placing these in that system.)

In certain email programs, if you put an @ in front of the folder name, it will keep that folder near the top of the list. In other email programs, you can drag them into position or make them favorites.

(If you have already implemented GTD to some degree, you may have already managed your email folder system appropriately for yourself. Great! Just use this jog to reassess whether it's working for you optimally, or if there's a simpler or more discretely organized way to have it make more sense for you.)

STOP HERE

Before you go further with the move, first create these folders in your email program and label them accordingly!

!

Empty Your Inbox Simulation

To practice, take a few minutes to go through the four sample items from an email inbox and decide what to do with each email.

EMAIL 1 OF 4 TO CLARIFY

Step 1. What is it?

    Subject line reads:

        Status Report for Friday's meeting

    Email body reads:

        Make sure you're up-to-date before our meeting by reading this report.

Step 2. Is it actionable?

☐ Yes
☐ No

Your Answer

Yes, it is actionable. If this were your email, you would add this task to your calendar since it needs to be done before Friday's meeting.

(Skip step 3 since it is actionable.)

Step 4. What's the next action?

Your Answer

Defer it by placing it in your email Next Actions folder, with a note on your calendar for the due-by date.

Step 1. What is it?

Subject line reads:

Bagels in the break room!

Email body reads:

They're on the counter if anyone wants them.

Step 2. Is it actionable?

☐ Yes

☐ No

Your Answer

Actually, either answer could be correct. If you want to get a bagel before they are gone, it is actionable!

If you don't want a bagel, it is not actionable. Delete the email and move on.

Step 1. What is it?

Subject line reads:

FYI—I won't be in today.

Email body reads:

To everyone in the office—I'm going to take the kids to the zoo today!
See you tomorrow. Hit me up on IM if you need me.

Step 2. Is it actionable?

☐ Yes
☐ No

Your Answer

No, this email is not actionable. It is an FYI—for your information.

Step 3. What do you do with it? *(Check one)*

☐ Delete it
☐ Incubate it in your Someday/Maybe folder
☐ Store it as reference material

Your Answer

Since it is just an FYI you can delete it. You are not waiting for any additional information from someone that you need to process, nor do you need to store it.

Step 1. What is it?

Subject line reads:
> **Your order has been successfully placed**

Email body reads:
> **Thank you for your order! You can track your shipment using #T315566218.**

Step 2. Is it actionable?

☐ Yes
☐ No

Your Answer

No, this email is not actionable.

Step 3. What do you do with it? *(Check one)*

☐ Delete it
☐ Incubate it in your Someday/Maybe folder
☐ Store it in your Waiting For folder

Your Answer

As you probably care that you receive the order, you'd place it in Waiting For, to be reviewed in case you need to follow up.

Now It's Your Turn

Open your email inbox and spend a few minutes practicing the Clarifying process you have just learned. Go through the questions for each email, determine if they're actionable, and decide what to do with them, using the step-by-step process.

STOP HERE

Before you go further, spend at least fifteen minutes working on getting your inbox to zero following the Clarifying process you have just learned.

FROM A GTD USER

"It was difficult for me at first to get my emails to empty. When I first started, I'd managed to process my emails down to the last dozen or so, but I wanted to keep them in my inbox because I was afraid I'd lose them. Finally I decided to start using my Next Actions folder for these emails. Now I can get my inbox to zero, and all my Next Action emails are in one place."

Frequently Asked Questions

Get Your Emails to Zero

Should I handle emails as soon as they come in?

This depends on your job. Many GTDers keep their email clients closed for most of the day. They'll check email intermittently—at the top of every hour, every other hour, or once in the morning and once in the afternoon—and handle the messages during those intervals. That way, their regular workflow isn't disrupted by incoming messages.

What if getting my inbox to zero is cutting into my planned work?

In a later move, we will discuss best practices for balancing planned work with new work that comes in every day. Most knowledge workers need ninety minutes each day to process their "Ins"—this includes physical and email incoming items.

Advanced Practices

Search vs. Reference Subfolders

Email search is becoming so powerful that many users rely on search to locate an email, rather than creating many subfolders under Reference. This saves you the time of creating subfolders, though categorizing your reference into discrete topics can be very useful. You decide what works best for you and your reference emails.

Congratulations!
You have successfully completed Move 5!

Go to the last page of the Workbook and update
Your Progress Tracker with today's date!

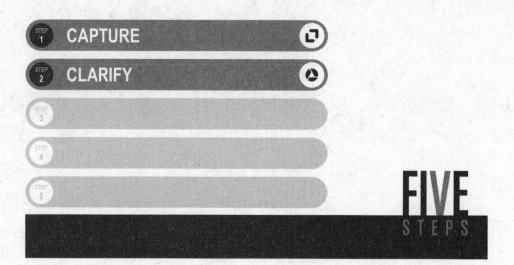

STEP 1 CAPTURE

STEP 2 CLARIFY

STEP 3

STEP 4

STEP 5

FIVE STEPS

Your Checklist for the Clarifying Moves

Move 4: Get Your In-tray to Empty

☐ I have followed the list of five steps to clarify everything in my in-tray.

Move 5: Get Your Emails to Zero

☐ I have followed the list of five steps to clarify everything in my email inbox.

Remember:

- Never put anything back in your in-tray after you have picked it up. Don't put it down until you've made a decision about it.
- Once you have opened an email, never close it without deciding what to do with it.
- Always start with the top item in your in-tray or inbox. Avoid the temptation to pick and choose items by looking through the stack for a "good one."

"If you are
appropriately engaged
with your life, you
don't need more time.
If you are not, more
time won't help."

—DAVID ALLEN

Create Your Next Actions and Other Lists

Why You Need This Move!

In the first three moves you worked on Capturing. You began writing down potentially actionable things as they came up in conversations, meetings, and even your own ideas. In the Clarifying moves, you determined next actions from all of those. The question remains, where do you put all these next actions you recognized?

This move provides the answer: you create a special list exactly for this purpose.

Keeping all of your next actions on a single list provides you with one place where you can keep track of what you need to do. These actions are how you make progress. They are the foundation unit for all of your productivity. Recording next actions and *keeping track* of them on one list, at least to begin with, is key to your success with GTD and stress-free productivity.

"Having three small children and running a business out of my home is an enormous challenge! It goes without saying that I'm prone to a lot of stress when so much is on my plate. Keeping my next actions on one list has really helped. I am the one to decide what goes on my Next Actions list—and what can be moved elsewhere, like onto my Someday/Maybe list. I feel much more organized and clearer-headed doing it this way."

Step-by-Step

Rather than simply learn about this move, it's best if you actually apply it as you go along. As you learn about each of the five steps in this move, put the Workbook aside and actually perform the actions as described. Then watch the magic unfold!

Step 1. Choose what you'll use for your GTD lists.

Step 2. Create a list and name it Next Actions.

Step 3. Capture the things you need to do as next actions on your list.

Step 4. Create your Someday/Maybe list.

Step 5. Create your Waiting For list.

Step 1. Choose what you'll use for your GTD lists.

If you already use a *smartphone, computer, or tablet* for making and keeping lists, we recommend that you continue using that same device for your Next Actions lists.

If you usually use *paper and pen,* we recommend that you continue using that for your Next Actions lists.

Yes, whatever you use currently for any kind of list, keep using that same tool for your Next Actions list. We want to keep this simple, especially at the beginning.

Is It Time to Change?

If you are thinking this is a good time to start using some new software or a new app, think again! Some people have the idea that starting GTD means using brand-new software or a cool app. Many apps do look appealing and seem just right for GTD. However, this is *not* the time to start using a new tool! Instead, it is vital that you focus on learning just one thing at a time. Keep your list as simple as you can for now. Wait until you are up to speed with GTD before trying a new app. This is a lesson learned from many before you: this is *not* the time to try out new software. Remember, you're learning a whole new way of managing your workflow. That is huge. Stick with whatever tool or software or app you currently use to make ordinary lists.

STOP HERE

Select Your ONE Next Action Tool

You may be currently using several different list tools. Use the following checklist to select the ONE you will start using from here on out for your Next Actions list.

1. Write down all the tools you use in the first column (for example, apps, a physical notebook, or document software such as Google Docs, Microsoft Word, or Pages).
2. Identify the one you are most used to and comfortable with.
3. Identify the one that is the simplest and most uncomplicated.
4. If it's a digital app, identify the one that can sync across all of your devices—computer, tablet, and smartphone.

1. Tool	2. Most Used	3. Simplest	4. Can Sync
Example: Evernote	X		X

Step 2. Create a list and name it Next Actions.

Create the list using the tool you have chosen, whether it is an app, software, or pen and paper.

Step 3. Capture the things you need to do as next actions on your list.

What is a next action?

A next action is the next, physical, visible activity that moves something toward completion. Everything you want to accomplish requires a next action to move it forward. Your next actions are the building blocks of your productivity.

How should you write a next action?

Start next actions with an *action verb*, for example:

- *Call* mechanic for car repair appointment
- *Take* phone to service shop for new screen
- *Take* kids to the aquarium
- *Buy* pasta for dinner
- *Call* the office about the project
- *Select* an outfit for the meeting
- *Read* the proposal

USE A SINGLE LIST

Writing down your next actions won't do much good unless you know exactly where the list is and you are able to get to it easily. A single list allows for a "one-stop shop" that you can quickly review at a glance. Later, we will discuss options for special purposes using more than a single list.

STOP HERE

Before you move on, put down this Workbook and turn your attention to your tool of choice, and take a few minutes to start your Next Actions list.

Next Actions vs. To-dos

When you identify something that you want or need to do, write it down as a next action. Next actions replace the older concept of to-dos—which are less specific. Using next actions also allows you to separate two things that too often run together:

1. Identifying something you want to complete.

and

2. Doing it.

When you write down next actions, you give yourself a chance to catch your breath. Later, you can look at your list and choose what you decide is best to work on now.

A typical to-do list includes items like "Dinner party," "Laundry," or "Day care." But there's a problem with how those items are written. **They're not actionable.** In your mind, you might have some action attached to the idea of "Dinner party," like "prepare" or "pick up." But these actions are in your head. The best practice is to get each action out of your head and make it explicit. Doing so makes a difference: No more thinking is required after you've written down these actions. Only the doing.

Write your next actions using active verbs at the beginning. These types of verbs command clear and specific *actions* that will give you the direction you need to complete them. Here are some examples of effective next action verbs:

Call . . .	Organize . . .	Review . . .
Buy . . .	Fill out . . .	Find . . .
Read . . .	Measure . . .	Talk to . . .
Purge . . .	Research . . .	Gather . . .
Print . . .	Take . . .	Wait for . . .
Load . . .	Draft . . .	Email . . .

Without a next action, there remains a potentially infinite gap between your current reality and what you need to do.

go.gettingthingsdone.com/no-10

Scan and learn more from David Allen about next actions.

+

Getting Things Done
the art of stress-free
productivity
from the **New York Times** bestselling author
David Allen

An all-new
updated
edition ✓

You can also find out more in chapter 12 of the GTD book.

Select a Verb for the Next Action

This exercise will help clarify next actions and the use of next action verbs. Look at the following next actions and the various action verbs. Which verb is clear and specific?

NEXT ACTION VERB #1

(Circle your choice of the action verb that is clear and specific.)

A Get in touch with Shantel

B Reach out to Shantel

C Call Shantel

Your Answer

A Get in touch with Shantel (Close, but vague.)

B Reach out to Shantel (Close, but vague.)

C Call Shantel (Yes. This verb is specific.)

NEXT ACTION VERB #2

(Circle your choice of the action verb that is clear and specific.)

A Go online and buy new running shoes

B Get new running shoes

C Shop for new running shoes

Your Answer

A Go online and buy new running shoes (Yes. Keep verbs brief and actionable.)

B Get new running shoes (Close, but vague with the use of "get.")

C Shop for new running shoes (Perhaps, depending on the outcome you want. Do you want to shop? Or do you want to buy new running shoes?)

NEXT ACTION VERB #3

(Circle your choice of the action verb that is clear and specific.)

A Review customer surveys

B Look at customer surveys

C Customer surveys

Your Answer

A Review customer surveys (Yes. The verb is precise and actionable.)

B Look at customer surveys (Is that all you need to do, look at them? Choose a more specific option.)

C Customer surveys (This is a common shortcut that is not a best practice. Writing a noun by itself is not sufficient; start with the action verb that is specific and actionable.)

Step 4. Create your Someday/Maybe list.

You are now aware that keeping track of next actions is essential for moving things forward. Those next actions are the items you have identified as important for you to do, as time allows.

You likely have other things you want to consider doing at some point. They are not certain enough or important enough to go on your Next Actions list. But you still want to capture those ideas when you get them so that they are off your mind. Remember: your mind is for *having* ideas, not *holding* them. Examples of Someday/Maybe items could include:

- Learn how artificial intelligence might affect your industry
- Start looking for a new home
- Research a new competitor
- Learn an instrument
- Update your LinkedIn profile
- Review online programs for a graduate degree

As you begin to use this new list, remember that someday/maybes are not throwaway items. They might actually end up being some of the most interesting and creative things you'll ever get involved with.

IMPORTANT! When you're ready to tackle an item that is on your Someday/Maybe list, decide on a next action and move that to your Next Actions list. And vice versa—if you decide that you're not going to take action on something that's already on your Next Actions list, move it to Someday/Maybe.

STOP HERE

Stop and do this now: take a few minutes to create your
Someday/Maybe list using the same tool you
selected for your Next Actions list.

Step 5. Create your Waiting For list.

The Waiting For list is for things you are expecting from someone else and allows you to keep track of the status of those things.

A Waiting For list item could be something you've delegated to someone, a sign-off on a project you have requested, or something you've ordered that hasn't yet arrived.

It's also helpful to add the date you started waiting, plus the due date, if there is one.

Examples of items on a Waiting For list—with the date that each was recorded:
- Miguel: Contract returned for the San Francisco venue—Nov. 14
- Melinda: Consultant expenses for marketing plans—Nov. 2
- Anthony: Carpeting from Home Depot: Order placed—Nov. 1
- Mom's doctor: Results from recent test—Nov. 3
- Accountant: Advice on travel deductions—Nov. 6

STOP HERE

Stop and do this now: take a few minutes to make
your Waiting For list using the same tool you
selected for your Next Actions list.

Your Calendar

Your calendar is likely the *most trusted part* of your current system. To keep it a trusted tool, the best practice is to use it for recording only *three kinds* of information.

1. **Time-specific actions**—Things that need to happen on a specific day and time. Example: *Team Meeting @ 8:45 a.m.*

A meeting is an example of a time-specific activity. These are most likely to be reliably on a person's calendar. Besides meetings, time-specific activities include:

- *Appointments*
- *Reserved time for a certain activity*

2. **Day-specific actions**—Things that need to happen during the day, but not at a specific time. Example: *Call James before EOD (end of day).*

A day-specific action could be a call you have to make before end of day. Other examples include:

- *An agenda you must prepare and distribute today, ahead of tomorrow's meeting*
- *A shipment that must be sent today*

3. **Day-specific information**—Information you want to know about that day or be reminded of on that day, not necessarily something to do. Example: *Miguel's birthday*. Other examples of day-specific information include:

- *Things that might disrupt your day (server shutdowns, office moves, etc.)*
- *External events to be aware of (big events in town, road closings, etc.)*
- *Activities of significant people in your life (family, coworkers, etc.)*

THE BIG "WATCH OUT!"

It is *not* a best practice to put next actions on your calendar that you'd simply *like* to do, because if you're unable to get them done that day, the calendar becomes less reliable—and you have to move your items to another day. Plus, you no longer have a single location for your next actions, which will come into play when you have time during the day. Consider your calendar to be the "hard landscape" of your day, the things that have to be done on a certain day, including meetings, deadlines, and day-specific events—the things you *have* to do, not things that you *want to try* to do. And if they are day- and time-specific, they do *not* go on your Next Actions list.

Frequently Asked Questions

Create Your Next Actions and Other Lists

Is there a correct way to sequence next actions on a list?

No, not really. If your list is too long, assess whether any could actually be moved to your Someday/Maybe list. You can also see "Advanced Practices" below and organize your lists by context.

How often should I check my calendar?

Typically, first thing in the morning, if not the day before, and as often as you need to in order to ensure that you are aware of what is upcoming. Some people go an extra step—they set an alarm on their smartphones ahead of meeting times and appointments.

How often should I review my lists?

You should review your Next Actions list when you have time available—to see what you can work on. When you do your GTD Weekly Review, you will review each of your lists and make sure they are current and useful.

Advanced Practices

Other Next Actions Lists

At some point, when you have identified all of your next actions, you may find that the volume of them can seem unwieldy to keep on one long list. If that's the case, you might consider subdividing your items into separate contexts, such as the specific location or tool required to perform the activity.

For instance, you might decide that keeping **Errands** on a separate list would make it easier to see them all when you go "out and about." Or keeping distinct lists for **At Office** and **At Home** might make more sense to you.

Again, keep your system as simple as possible in the beginning, and then allow yourself to experiment with ways to customize it to your specific inclinations.

Congratulations!
You have successfully completed Move 6!

Go to the last page of the Workbook and update
Your Progress Tracker with today's date!

"The essence of Getting Things Done is knowing what "done" means, and what "doing" looks like and where it happens; and this data almost never shows up by itself. It requires thinking—not a lot, but more than you think."

— DAVID ALLEN

Keep Track of Your Projects on One List

Why You Need This Move!

So you have a handful of lists in place where you can capture all of your next actions or other actions like "Someday/Maybe" or "Waiting For." Projects are the next level up from *actions*. You may have *many* personal and professional projects going on at the same time that you need to stay on top of. This move is about keeping track of those projects.

What Is a Project?

Simply put, a project is anything you need or want to do that requires *more than one action step*, and that you can accomplish within about a year. Because identifying projects is so important to completing things, you need a simple and precise way to keep track of them: your Projects list.

What Is a Projects List?

A Projects list is an inventory of your current projects. Maintaining a list of your projects helps you stay organized and saves time by giving you rapid access to your list of projects. This best practice will help you to complete things and reduce your stress.

What Goes on Your Projects List?

Think about all of the multistep tasks you want to complete in the next year—from finishing the quarterly report, to reorganizing your department, to furnishing your child's room, to learning to ski the advanced slopes. Large or small, they're all multistep projects, and they deserve space on your list. Example of a Projects list:

Research relationship w/ J. Smith, Inc.

Implement new fiscal year budget

Get new car

Hire marketing director

Update business directory

Install new software infrastructure

Projects List vs. Next Actions List

You may be asking yourself: "What is the difference between a Projects list and a Next Actions list? Can't I just use one or the other instead of having both?"

Not quite. Though both lists help you stay on top of your work, each serves a different purpose.

Your Next Actions list identifies the single, specific, next physical action you will take. On the other hand, your Projects list identifies your desired outcomes that *will require more than one next action* and could take up to a year to accomplish.

In other words, your Projects list captures the desired outcomes for each of your current projects, while your Next Actions list tracks individual next actions, both those that will contribute to a project and those that stand alone.

On average, most people tend to have between twenty and one hundred current projects on their plate at any given time. You may be surprised to find that you have more projects than you think!

Step-by-Step

Step 1. Create a Projects list.

Step 2. Populate your Projects list.

Step 3. State each project in terms of the desired outcome and begin with a final outcome verb.

Step 4. Write at least one next action for each project.

Step 1. Create a Projects list.

In the tool you selected in Move 6, create a list and label it "Projects List."

THE POWER OF PROJECTS LISTS

A current and complete list of your projects is one of the most important lists for you to maintain. It gives you a quick snapshot of your commitments over the next twelve months or so. It includes projects you want to do, and the projects you believe you "have to do," personally or professionally.

Your Projects list doesn't need to be complicated. Simply list the name of each project, stated as a desired outcome, along with at least one associated next action.

Making a Projects list can be challenging. For many of us, it can be a source of anxiety, especially the first time. However, it turns out that listing your projects—and making them more visible to you—allows you to begin to gain a greater sense of control. You will start to see all that you have committed to, which in turn will allow you to decide what you should delete, renegotiate, or put more effort into.

> **You can only feel comfortable about what you're not doing**
> **when you know what you're not doing.**
>
> **—DAVID ALLEN**

Step 2. Populate your Projects list.

Now that you have your Projects list, it is time to add projects to it. On the following pages in the Workbook you'll have some time for reflection which will result in items that you can transfer onto your new Projects list.

GOALS AND OBJECTIVES

Your current work goals and objectives that can be finished within a year are often projects. Capture them below:

1. _____

2. _____

3. _____

4. _____

5. _____

6. _____

7. _____

8. _____

Review the items you listed above. Circle the ones that are projects and add them to your Projects list.

CURRENT ACTIVITIES

Your calendar, your Next Actions list, your Waiting For list, and your work space are bound to trigger reminders of projects you have to complete. Take a moment to review these lists and places and list what you discover below:

1. _____
2. _____
3. _____
4. _____
5. _____
6. _____
7. _____

Review the items you listed above. Circle the ones that are projects and add them to your Projects list.

CAREER GOALS

What are your career goals? What do you want to accomplish in your professional life? List your thoughts below:

1. _____

2. _____

3. _____

4. _____

Review the items you listed above. Are any of these to be accomplished within the next year? If so, circle them, decide if you want to make them a project, and add them to your Projects list. Others that remain can go on your Someday/Maybe list.

PROBLEMS

We all face problems. The very nature of being alive and living in the world results in situations we are not satisfied with and that we identify as problems. In the space below, list several problems you are currently facing.

1. _____

2. _____

3. _____

4. _____

5. _____

6. _____

7. _____

One of the keystone principles of GTD is to **view problems as projects**. When you have identified a problem, reframe it and re-label it as a project. Voilà! It now suggests that there is a solution to be had and that it can be achieved by taking action. The solution to the problem becomes the desired outcome of the project.

DESIRED OUTCOME

For each of the problems you listed on the previous page, restate it in the spaces below as a project. Remember: Always state a project in terms of the desired outcome.
This becomes the name of that project.

1. _____

2. _____

3. _____

4. _____

5. _____

6. _____

7. _____

8. _____

Review the desired outcomes you listed above. Circle the ones that you want to add to
your Projects list. Others that remain can go on your Someday/Maybe list.

SELF-IMPROVEMENT

When you think about self-improvement, what comes to mind? Are there aspects of your life that you would like to change? Is there some outcome you want in your personal or professional life? Add any items that come to mind below. (No, you don't need to fill in all six. And yes, you can add more if you care to. It's your life, and there is no time like the present!) State each one as a desired outcome.

1. _____

2. _____

3. _____

4. _____

5. _____

6. _____

Review the items you listed above. Circle the ones that you want to take on as a project and add them to your Projects list. Others that remain can go on your Someday/Maybe list.

CREATIVE EXPRESSION

Are there any interests you would like to develop? Cooking, drawing, coding, knitting? List these interests below and add the ones you select to your Projects list. Others that remain can go on your Someday/Maybe list.

1. _____

2. _____

3. _____

4. _____

5. _____

Step 3. State each project in terms of the desired outcome and begin with a final outcome verb.

DESIRED OUTCOME

Go through the list of projects you created and ensure that each one is stated in terms of the desired outcome. This is the bigger, better, faster, easier end result you want.

Examples of desired outcomes:

- Complete the office reorganization
- Implement new fiscal year budget
- Complete the research on w/J. Smith Inc.
- Buy new car (Technically, the desired outcome is to own the new car, while the activity required to produce the result is to "buy" the new car.)
- Hire Marketing Director (Same. Technically, the desired outcome is have the new person on board, while the activity required to produce the result is to "hire" the person.)

ACTION VERBS

It also works to state it in terms of *the action required to produce the desired outcome*, such as complete, update, organize, purchase, implement, etc. You may recall something similar for your Next Actions list. Unlike the Next Actions verbs, those on your Projects list need to indicate the conclusion of *multiple steps*.

Here are some examples of effective project action verbs:

Finalize . . .	Resolve . . .	Set up . . .
Organize . . .	Submit . . .	Maximize . . .
Ensure . . .	Reorganize . . .	Publish . . .
Update . . .	Design . . .	Complete . . .
Install . . .	Roll out . . .	Implement . . .

go.gettingthingsdone.com/no-11

Scan and learn more from David Allen about writing effective project definitions.

+

You can also find out more in chapter 7 of the GTD book.

Step 4. Write at least one next action for each project.

Now that you have created a list of all of your projects in a Projects list, there is one more step to this move—always write a next action for each project. This is the project's *first, most immediate*, next action. Doing this ensures that you have a reminder on your list that's going to move the project forward.

You can *do* next actions, but you can't "do" a project. You can only perform the actions it requires, starting with the first logical action.

Examples:

Project/Desired Outcome (What's the larger result desired? How will you know when it is done?)	Next Action (What do you need to do that? Do you have everything you need?)
Complete the office reorganization	Call Susan re: source for filing cabinets
Implement new fiscal year budget	Email Bill for copy of last year's budget
Research relationship w/ J. Smith Inc.	Draft proposal ideas for alliance
Get new car	Research web sources—cars
Hire marketing director	Talk to Sean re: job description

!

PRACTICE: SELECT THE NEXT ACTION FOR A PROJECT

Take a look at the following projects and practice identifying what you think the next action should be.

Project #1: Repair your car.

What's the next action for this project? (*Circle your choice.*)

A. Think about alternative ways to get to work.

B. Save money for the repairs.

C. Call the mechanic.

Your Answer

A. Think about alternative ways to get to work.
That may be important to do, but it does not move this project forward. Try another option.

B. Save money for the repairs.
Yes, if you know it will cost more money than you have right now.

C. Call the mechanic.
Yes, this may be the next specific action required to fix the car.

Project #2: Complete the proposal you promised by next Friday.

What's the next action for this project? (*Circle your choice.*)

A. Write the proposal.

B. Draft an outline.

C. Estimate a budget.

Your Answer

A. Write the proposal.

This could be the next action, if this is not really a project. (Projects have multiple actions required to complete them.) Try another option.

B. Draft an outline.

Yes, this may be the logical next action to take for completing the proposal.

C. Estimate a budget.

Yes, this may be the logical next action to take for completing the proposal.

Project #3: Paint the living room.

What's the next action for this project? (*Circle your choice.*)

A. Visit paint shop to pick out a desired color for the walls.

B. Think of friends to help you paint.

C. Consider whether to buy new furniture.

Your Answer

A. Visit paint shop to pick out a desired color for the walls.

Yes, that is a possible next action for painting the living room.

B. Think of friends to help you paint.

But how would you get them to engage? A bit too vague as a next action for painting the living room.

C. Consider whether to buy new furniture.

That may be a separate action or project, but it does not move this project forward. Try another next action for this project.

Project #4: Learn WordPress for building your website.

What's the next action for this project? (*Circle your choice.*)

A. Find online resources to learn WordPress.

B. Find out if your company will reimburse you.

C. Sign up for the class that teaches WordPress.

Your Answer

A. Find online resources to learn WordPress.
Yes, this could be the next action for this project.

B. Find out if your company will reimburse you.
Not a specific action named yet. How would you find out?

C. Sign up for the class that teaches WordPress.
Yes, this could be the next action for this project, as long as you know where to sign up.

Frequently Asked Questions

Keep Track of Your Projects on One List

Can I have multiple Projects lists?

If you need to have multiple Projects lists, feel free. Some people prefer one for work and one for personal use. However, one list may be the best way to go because it serves as a master inventory, one place you can reliably see all your projects. See "Advanced Practices" on p. 154.

What about delegated projects?

You may have projects you want completed but you have handed all or part of them to someone else—someone who reports to you, for example, or a family member. In those instances, you may want a **Projects: Delegated** list to track them. In that scenario, your GTD Weekly Review should include that list and possible next actions to follow up with those delegated projects.

What if some of my projects require their own subprojects to complete?

You can break out large projects into subprojects or list them separately as projects. The truth is, it doesn't really matter. You should do what you're most comfortable with. As long as you're regularly reviewing your Projects list, you'll be able to stay current.

FROM A GTD USER

"At one point, I had over 140 items on my Projects list! I knew I was overcommitted, but I didn't know what to do. At least each project had a clear outcome and a next action step. However, I realized that I simply wasn't going to complete all of my projects. This was hard for me, but at the same time a huge relief. To make it manageable, I chose the projects that had the most meaning for me, and narrowed my list down to 60 manageable projects. Some of them I decided I would never do and others I moved to my Someday/Maybe list. Much better."

Advanced Practices Other Projects Lists

Once you have mastered your use of your Projects list, you might want to create sections within your Projects list, or separate Projects lists. Here are some examples of these.

1. Personal/Professional Lists. Some people feel more comfortable seeing their lists divided between personal and professional projects. You'll need to review your Personal list as closely as you would your Professional list—and don't save the Personal list just for the weekends! Often, some of the greatest pressures on professionals stem from personal aspects of their lives that they let slip.

2. Delegated Projects. As we mentioned in the "Frequently Asked Questions" section, you can create a **Projects: Delegated** list to track projects you have assigned to someone else. Remember to review this list and follow up regularly to make sure everything is moving along appropriately.

3. Specific Types of Projects. In some instances, you may find it valuable to group together several different projects of the same type. For example, you might have a category called **Projects: Presentations** with a chronological listing of all of your upcoming events that center around presentations. In this case, you'd review this list for actions until they are completed as you would for other Projects lists, but it might be helpful to see them all on one list, in the order they are scheduled on your calendar, apart from your other projects.

4. Creating Subprojects. Some of your projects will likely have major subordinate projects, each of which might be seen as an entire project in its own right. If you make a large project a single listing on your Projects list, you'll need to keep a list of the subprojects and/or the project plan itself as "project support material" that you can review when you come to that major project. This technique is recommended if big pieces of the project are dependent on other pieces being completed first. In this case, you might have subprojects with no next actions attached to them. This is because these actions are waiting for other things to happen before they can move forward. As an example, you might not be able to start on "Upgrade the kitchen" until you've finished "Assess and upgrade home electrical system." Or perhaps you can afford only one of your major home projects at a time, so keeping them lined up in order of your priorities would make sense. However, you might give "Finalize the patio" the go-ahead independently of the other subprojects. In this case, you'd want a next action to be continually current on this larger project to make progress on it independently.

Congratulations!
You have successfully completed Move 7!

Go to the last page of the Workbook and update
Your Progress Tracker with today's date!

"Some people have lists of big goals and visions, and many people have lists of simple to-dos. Very few have a list of all the in-between outcomes (i.e., "projects"), and that's a critical list for staying focused on the right stuff, week to week."

—DAVID ALLEN

Create Folders to Stay Organized

Why You Need This Move!

You need this move **IF** you have ever asked:

- "Where is that form . . . ?"
- "I wonder what I did with that paper. . . ."
- "Could you please resend that file . . . ?"
- "Where did I put that email?"

Being disorganized is one of life's biggest stressors. It also takes away from being productive.

Staying organized with folders is a valuable time saver, frustration saver, and stress saver! The system you are about to implement in your life allows you to quickly **store** information in an organized way and to quickly **access** it when needed. You will find it to be flexible, complete, and expandable for all of your reference and support materials.

This move is all about creating a simple and manageable way to organize your papers and files.

Step-by-Step

Step 1. Go shopping for supplies.

Step 2. Set up your paper folders.

Step 3. Set up your digital folders.

Step 1. Go shopping for supplies.

Yes, even if you have created digital lists using an app, there are still some things you need to do manually. So here's what you need:

☐ **A box of folders**—Obtain a box of new, third-cut, two-ply top-file folders. Avoid using hanging folders, if possible. If you must use the hanging type, put only a couple of folders inside each hanger and label the manila folders instead of the hanging ones.

☐ **A–Z preprinted labels or A–Z dividers**—You can find preprinted file dividers to help organize your reference materials. Alternatively, you can use preprinted labels. Obviously, for all folders with names beginning with *A*, you will place them behind your folder with the preprinted *A*. Examples include *Accountant* and *Auto*. Repeat for folders *B* through *Z*.

☐ **A box of blank labels (for handwritten labels) or, better yet, a label maker**—You can use either blank labels or a label maker. A label maker is a very good investment! It keeps your files clean and easy to navigate. (You will be amazed at how good this feels! You will immediately feel more organized.)

☐ **A filing cabinet, drawers, or portable filing system that can hold the folders**—You may want to arrange for new file drawers, or purchase a filing cabinet. Be sure to select ones with high-quality mechanics. This is not the place to skimp on quality.

STOP HERE

Before moving on, make sure you have all of the supplies from the previous page on hand.

Step 2. Set up your paper folders.

With the supplies in front of you, create folders for all of the following and drop them alphabetically into your filing cabinet or portable system. This may take up to an hour, so plan accordingly.

- [ ] **Next Actions Support Folder**—This will hold information and documents that help you to complete the items on your Next Actions list. This includes notes to self, backup documents, brochures, schedules, or whatever you will need to complete that next action. It is usually simpler and faster to have one folder for all of these items rather than creating a separate folder for each item.

- [ ] **Project Folders**—Each of your projects that may have relevant collateral materials should have its own folder—the label is the name of the project. These folders hold all of the reference and support material for your work on these projects. They include material that's not immediately actionable—things like schedules, planning documents, meeting notes, examples from other projects, lists of ideas, and other items. Some people prefer to keep their Project folders closer to hand—on their desk or in front of their file drawer.

- [ ] **A–Z Folders**—These folders contain any nonactionable reference material and information you want or need to keep track of. This may include articles, receipts, contracts, and other documents—items you might need to access later. You should create a unique folder for each topic or category, depending on your needs. Arrange them alphabetically so that you can look in only one or two places to find what you need.

- [ ] **Waiting for Support Folder**—This file is where you place reminders of items you're waiting for. This includes items detailing delegation, requests of others, receipts for items ordered, and the like. Keep these items listed on your Waiting For list, as this folder merely holds collateral materials you might need for follow-up.

- [ ] **To Home Folder**—Anything that needs transport from the office to your home goes into this folder. This one may live in your briefcase or in a designated spot in your office.

- [ ] **To Office Folder**—The things that need transport to the office from home go in this folder. This one may live in your briefcase, purse, or in a designated spot in your home.

STOP HERE

Before moving on, make sure you have created all of your folders and arranged them alphabetically in your filing system of choice.

Step 3. Set up your digital folders.

When it comes to the files on your computer you can follow a similar process to organize your digital files. You will find it helpful to have a parallel system for your paper and for your digital documents.

☐ For Email—Create the following email folders and place them at the top of your list of folders:
  ■ *Next Actions*
  ■ *Waiting For*
  ■ *Separate folders for any project that has relevant emails*

☐ Instead of A–Z folders for all the other emails you want to keep, another option is to keep one single Archive folder. Email programs now provide excellent search capabilities. When you need to locate a specific email, use the search box for the sender, the receiver, or the subject.

To take advantage of this, instead of creating A–Z folders and filing each email that you want to keep, bypass that process entirely. Set up a folder for storage and label it with the current year, such as "20xx." (You can use the year and quarter if you have a very high number of emails you want to keep, such as "20xx Q1.")

With some email programs, you can place an "@" symbol or some other character in front of the name for any folder you want to keep at the top of your list of folders.

TIPS FOR CREATING A FUSS-FREE PAPER FILE SYSTEM

BEST PRACTICE	NOT RECOMMENDED
Filing drawers that are only two-thirds full allow for easy access and keep your filing and retrieval fast and easy.	Packed filing drawers make it hard and unpleasant to file—and difficult to locate your documents.
Use only one system for organizing folders.	Multiple file systems, or color-coded files. This is too complicated to maintain!
Keep new and unused folders and labels waiting close by. Make sure these supplies are within an arm's length of your desk chair.	No blank folders at hand.
Use more drawers as needed if files grow. Prune your files at least yearly.	Old and outdated papers and files clogging the drawer.
Use a label maker instead of handwritten labels.	Handwritten tabs are hard to read and don't give the same level of satisfaction.
Folders are easier to add quickly. If you must use hanging files, avoid the plastic tabs; simply label the folders and place only one inside each hanging file.	Hanging files and plastic-tabbed labels are too much trouble to use.

Frequently Asked Questions

Create Folders to Stay Organized

What if I have to use the hanging files at work?

Most desk file drawers are built for hanging files, and some companies require hanging files. We recommend that you put only one or two files inside each hanger and label the initial file instead of the hanging file. This makes it much easier to see and find the files, and allows an A–Z system to work better without fighting with over-stuffed hangers.

Why is a labeler important?

Typeset labels using a labeler keep your system attractive and efficient. You would be amazed at the number of people who tell me what a difference this makes for them, having cleaner, clearer file labels! You will find it to be worth the time, effort, and money.

Are there any brands or supply stores you recommend?

There's only one recommendation: quality. Don't skimp here. You're looking for sturdy, resilient folders. Use a strong cabinet. Look for the most durable supplies at the best price.

Why use A–Z alphabetical labels? Can I color-code instead?

Color-coding looks pretty, but it becomes a pain when you're creating new files and needing to keep an inventory of each color. Believe me, alphabetizing is the only system that holds up over any significant length of time. It's fast and easy.

How often should I purge my files?

Purge them as often as you need to to keep your system attractive and efficient. You don't want your filing system to become a junk drawer. Go through your files on at least a yearly basis and toss anything you no longer need. Straighten the papers. Replace folders that are tearing or worn.

Advanced Practices

Use a Tickler File

A tickler file is a set of folders with future dates. The purpose is to have the materials available on the day they are needed. Examples include notes for an upcoming meeting, travel documents, or a birthday card purchased for someone.

Typical Setup

1. Have a section in your file drawer labeled "Tickler Files."
2. Get a stack of folders and number them 1 through 31, representing each day of the month.
3. Behind those folders, label twelve folders with the name of each month. This provides a year of folders.

To Use

1. As time passes and you have paper that you will need on a particular date, file it in the folder for that month.
2. On the first of each month, remove the items from that month's folder and sort them into the daily (1–31) folders.
3. Retrieve the information for a given day when needed. Note: Make sure you note in your calendar that the needed paper for a scheduled event is in your tickler file.

This type of system is also referred to as a perpetual file, bring-forward file, follow-up file, or suspense file.

Digital Triggers

You may prefer to use your digital calendar for this "tickler" function, using the day-specific information aspect of the calendar to remind you about something on a particular date. If so, and if there is relevant physical material, keep that in your paper-based filing system, which your digital note will remind you to find.

Create a Read and Review Folder

You will no doubt discover in your in-tray a number of things for which your next action is to read. These printed items that will demand more than two minutes are best managed by placing them in a separate stacking tray or folder labeled **Read/ Review**. You can have both a physical and digital version of this folder.

Tips for Getting to Your Reading

☐ Carry some of these items with you to fill the time when waiting on a meeting.

☐ Take them with you on trains or planes.

☐ Set regular time on your calendar or write a next action if needed to ensure required reading occurs.

Congratulations!
You have successfully completed Move 8!

Go to the last page of the Workbook and update
Your Progress Tracker with today's date!

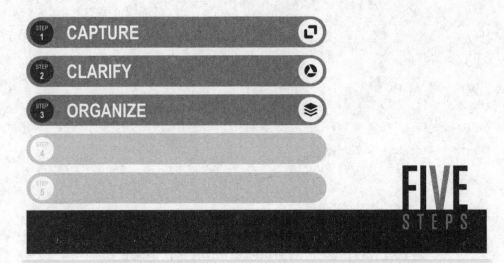

STEP 1 CAPTURE

STEP 2 CLARIFY

STEP 3 ORGANIZE

STEP 4

STEP 5

FIVE
STEPS

Your Checklist for the Organizing Moves

Move 6

☐ I have created a Next Actions list.

☐ I keep track of my next actions on one or an appropriate number of lists.

☐ I have created a Someday/Maybe list.

☐ I have created a Waiting For list (to keep track of things that I've handed off to someone else).

Move 7

☐ I have created a Projects list.

☐ I keep track of my projects on one or an appropriate number of lists.

Move 8

☐ I have created paper folders to organize my projects and support materials.

☐ I have set up my paper A–Z reference system using folders.

☐ I have set up my digital reference system on my computer.

Calendars

☐ I use my calendar only for the following activities:

- *Date-specific activities*
- *Time-specific activities*
- *Reminders for that day*

" Being organized simply means that where something is matches what it means to you. I'm not a naturally organized person—I'm a naturally lazy person! And I'm only organized so that I don't have to continually rethink what something means to me. If it's on that list, in that folder, in that drawer, it means *X*, and I don't have to rethink it, other than to choose whether to engage with it or not. **"**

— DAVID ALLEN

Do a GTD Weekly Review

Why You Need This Move!

A GTD Weekly Review consists of sitting down, perhaps at the same time and place, and reviewing your past week, your upcoming week(s), and your GTD system. If you are like most people, this will become one of the most trusted and satisfying activities of your week.

Just like a chef sharpens his knives, and a race car driver tunes her engine, we all need to take time to renew, review, and be more productive—in our work and in our personal life.

You picked up this Workbook because you wanted to be more productive and reduce stress. As you learn to implement these moves in your life, especially the GTD Weekly Review, you'll do both.

Your GTD Weekly Review will help you to recognize what you've been accomplishing, and what you have yet to implement, in your movement toward more productivity with less stress, both in your work and in your personal life. Doing your review is essential for finding balance in your work and life.

Every Week?

Do you really have to do a GTD Weekly Review every week? No, you don't have to. It is always a choice. You may find, though, that it becomes like brushing your teeth: if you don't do it, you feel grungy and out of sorts. It is a best practice, embraced by those who want to be more productive, with less stress. You may find that, like meditating or getting a massage, it is a calming, centering, and grounding activity you look forward to each week. It is your time to restore and refresh.

COMMENTS FROM GTD USERS

The Weekly Review is all about habit building. Here are a few ideas from experienced users to help kick-start it.

Attach it to another activity—"I read that every habit is triggered by something else—a daily event, a time of day, a routine. So I linked my Weekly Review to my Saturday breakfast. I do it while I eat and I never miss my GTD Weekly Review—or a Saturday breakfast."

Make it easy to do—"I saw the need to build a new habit. I made the process as easy as I could when I got started. I keep it focused, and now I can't live without it."

Build a record of consecutive wins—"It took me awhile to develop the GTD Weekly Review habit. I used to call it my Monthly GTD Weekly Review! Now I love the time I take on Sunday afternoons in my home office to review my system. I put on my favorite music, Yo-Yo Ma or Rosa Passos, and spend the time to get clean and current with my work and my personal life. It is my time to see what I've missed, and to reflect and renew."

Decide on a reward—"It sounds silly, but promising myself a reward motivates me to complete my review. Something as simple as an ice cream cone or fifteen minutes of a fun activity works for me."

Track your progress—"I use the progress tracking chart to record my GTD Weekly Reviews. It gives me a way to monitor my progress visually and see my habit develop, week after week."

Location, location—"I had trouble fitting a GTD Weekly Review into my life. I have children, and I work in a busy office. I had no time—or place—without interruptions. Then one day, while driving to work, I noticed the public library. No interruptions! Plenty of quiet! Now once a week I leave early and stop at the library to spend time away from the world, reviewing my Projects and Next Actions lists. This time has had a huge positive impact on my productivity—and in reducing my stress."

Step-by-Step

Step 1. Conduct your first GTD Weekly Review.

Step 2. Choose a regular time and place, and schedule it on your calendar.

Step 1. Conduct your first GTD Weekly Review.

Since there is no better time than the present, and you already have your Workbook open and have progressed this far in the process, take time now to complete your first GTD Weekly Review.

We've made this easy for you. All you have to do is go through the GTD Weekly Review Checklist on the next page, one item at a time. As you do, you'll notice that you are already familiar with the principles and practices—it's what you've been doing all along!

PRINT IT!

You have permission—and are encouraged—to duplicate the GTD Weekly Review Checklist to use each week. If you are not near a photocopier, you can take a picture with your smartphone, paste the photo into a document, and print the document.

GTD Weekly Review Checklist

Get Clear

☐ Collect loose papers and materials
  Gather all accumulated business cards, receipts, and miscellaneous paper-based materials into your in-tray.

- ☐ Get your "In" to zero

  Process completely all outstanding paper materials, journal and meeting notes, voicemails, dictation, and emails.
- ☐ Empty your head

  Put in writing and process any uncaptured new projects, action items, waiting-fors, someday/maybes, etc.

Get Current

- ☐ Review Next Actions lists

  Mark off completed actions. Review for reminders of further action steps to record.
- ☐ Review previous calendar data

  Review past calendar in detail for remaining items, reference data, etc., and transfer into the active system.
- ☐ Review upcoming calendar

  Review upcoming calendar events—long- and short-term. Capture actions triggered.
- ☐ Review Waiting For list

  Record appropriate actions for any needed follow-up. Check off received ones.
- ☐ Review Projects (and larger outcome) lists

  Evaluate status of projects, goals, and outcomes, one by one, ensuring at least one current next action item on each. Browse through project plans, support material, and any other work-in-progress material to trigger new actions, completions, waiting-fors, etc.
- ☐ Review any relevant checklists

  Use as a trigger for any new actions.

Get Creative

- ☐ Review Someday/Maybe list

  Review for any projects or actions that may now have become active, and transfer to the appropriate list. Delete items no longer of interest.
- ☐ Be creative and courageous

  Add any new, wonderful, hare-brained, creative, thought-provoking, or risk-taking ideas into your system.

Step 2. Choose a regular time and place, and schedule it on your calendar.

1. Time. Choose a day and time of the week that works for you—a time you are most likely to stick to, week after week. Some people prefer early Friday afternoons, or sometime on Saturday or Sunday, when they can get away by themselves for some quiet and reflect. The key is to pick a day and time for this that you believe you can make a habit.

2. Place. Select a good place to conduct your review, ideally somewhere quiet with no distractions. An obvious place is your office or home, but make sure you can be undisturbed. This time is for *you*. Many people like to have a getaway location, such as a coffee shop, a park, or a library, specifically for the GTD Weekly Review. Consider putting your phone on airplane mode during this time.

3. Calendar. Open your calendar and write "GTD Weekly Review" on your chosen day and time, and make it a weekly "repeating "event. Start with only thirty minutes in order to make building the habit easier. You can add more time in later weeks, ten minutes or so at a time. Avoid the tendency to do a marathon review in the first few months: it can leave you feeling mentally spent and with less of a desire to do another. Schedule this appointment with yourself and make it a recurring appointment. *Guard this time—it is time you sanction for yourself!*

4. Repeat. You've started on the road to stress-free productivity—now make it a habit by doing it each and every week, and watch as you keep getting better at getting things done. You need to do what you need to do to conduct your review each week. You may be tempted to skip it one time because of the crush of . . . everything. That is the point. This is the time to reflect on all that, find ways to make it better for yourself, and make certain your system is in good repair.

5. Instill. Here's a great way to instill the habit: pick a friend you can report progress with. Sending a simple message or text with "yes" or "no" can keep you motivated to complete it.

STOP HERE

Before moving on, make sure you have *scheduled* your repeating Weekly Review on your calendar, or else it will likely not get done!

Frequently Asked Questions

Do a GTD Weekly Review

How much time should I spend on each step of a GTD Weekly Review?

Take as much time as you need, and as long as you are receiving value from it.

Should I do two separate reviews, one for work and one for personal?

This is not recommended. It's hard enough to find the time to do one, so limit it to one once per week, and cover it all.

What if I fall behind or miss a GTD Weekly Review?

That means you are part of normal life today! Don't make it wrong or bad. Think of your reviews as a gift you give yourself. Then complete the next one as soon as you can—to get back on track. You will likely find that, after doing your reviews for a while, you will be very aware if you skip it. Like skipping taking a shower, you will notice the discomfort and take the needed action.

The Weekly Review Checklist is a long form. The first few weeks, do only a portion of it—about thirty minutes' worth. It will leave you hungry for more next week.

The GTD Weekly Review is the single most important move for consistent GTD practice. If you do it, your system will live and grow more mature and meaningful. If you don't, your practice will diminish and eventually fall away.

—DAVID ALLEN

Congratulations!
You have successfully completed Move 9!

Go to the last page of the Workbook and update
Your Progress Tracker with today's date!

STEP 1 **CAPTURE**

STEP 2 **CLARIFY**

STEP 3 **ORGANIZE**

STEP 4 **REFLECT**

STEP 5

FIVE STEPS

Your Reflecting Checklist Is Also Your Weekly Review Checklist

Get Clear

☐ Collect loose papers and materials

Gather all accumulated business cards, receipts, and miscellaneous paper-based materials into your in-tray.

☐ Get your "In" to zero

Process completely all outstanding paper materials, journal and meeting notes, voicemails, dictation, and emails.

☐ Empty your head

Put in writing and process any uncaptured new projects, action items, waiting-fors, someday/maybes, etc.

Get Current

☐ Review Next Actions lists
Mark off completed actions. Review for reminders of further action steps to record.

☐ Review previous calendar data
Review past calendar in detail for remaining items, reference data, etc., and transfer into the active system.

☐ Review upcoming calendar
Review upcoming calendar events—long- and short-term. Capture actions triggered.

☐ Review Waiting For list
Record appropriate actions for any needed follow-up. Check off received ones.

☐ Review Projects (and larger outcome) lists
Evaluate status of projects, goals, and outcomes, one by one, ensuring at least one current next action item on each. Browse through project plans, support material, and any other work-in-progress material to trigger new actions, completions, waiting-fors, etc.

☐ Review any relevant checklists
Use as a trigger for any new actions.

Get Creative

☐ Review Someday/Maybe list
Review for any projects or actions that may now have become active, and transfer to the appropriate list. Delete items no longer of interest.

☐ Be creative and courageous
Add any new, wonderful, hare-brained, creative, thought-provoking, or risk-taking ideas into your system.

"Most people feel best about their work the week before they take a big holiday. It's not about the holiday—it's because they're rethinking, recalibrating, and renegotiating all their commitments so they can be free on the beach, on the slopes, or hiking in the woods. I just suggest doing that weekly, not yearly."

— DAVID ALLEN

Conduct a Daily Review

Why You Need This Move!

You're a knowledge worker in a fast-changing world. Your work involves making split-second *judgments* and managing all the ongoing data and information coming at you. While your job may define much of what you do, ultimately, your life, your career, what you achieve, and what you decide to do today are *up to you*. The GTD system you've created so far in this Workbook will help you live a stress-free, productive life.

This final move is the capstone move that takes all you've learned so far and gives you necessary guidance for tackling the day-to-day demands on your time and mind.

WHAT DAVID IS SAYING

"Having a clear head and relaxed, focused control is dependent on orienting yourself in space and time with the appropriate 'maps'—i.e., the lists and pictures of your landscape of commitments and interests. The real value of building a trusted external brain, as GTD does, is to free you to make good, intuitive choices about what to be doing, moment to moment."

MOVE 10
Step-by-Step

Step 1. Review your calendar first.

Step 2. Do an "emergency scan."

Step 3. Check your lists.

Step 4. Set aside "clarifying time."

Step 5. Identify and address your limiting criteria.

Step 1. Review your calendar first.

Review the *hard landscape* of your day. This includes what you have committed to, such as meetings, appointments, certain deliverables—the things that *have to be handled* sometime that day. Also include anything you just need to be aware of about the day.

Step 2. Do an "emergency scan."

Next, do an "emergency scan" of your new inputs to see if there is anything that must be taken care of right away. Keep in mind this is a quick scan—five minutes, ten minutes tops. The challenge is to avoid getting distracted by what's in there—you will have time later to Clarify and Organize your email and other communications, as part of your "planned work." Your job now is only to check for emergency items.

Step 3. Check your lists.

Check your Next Actions list(s). Consider the actions you can take in your current context (this will be explained shortly) with the time you have available, or those you need to add to your items for later today. Some people like to use a "punch list" for this purpose. This is a short list of what would be most valuable to deal with, if you have the time.

Step 4. Set aside "clarifying time."

This is the time required to take care of and clarify the items in your "In," as you learned in Step 2: Clarifying earlier. This is when you set aside, or block out, or at least recognize that you need time on your calendar for this crucial activity. Consider appropriate "processing time" you'll need during the day to deal with your "In" and new incoming content, so you don't overcommit yourself.

STOP HERE

Before moving on, conduct a quick review by following steps
1 through 4 from the previous pages. Don't take long,
just get a sense for what the process feels like.

How Much Time a Day Do I Need?

A typical working professional, perhaps like you, needs sixty to ninety minutes a day to stay on top of what has already come in—to clarify and to deal with all the email and other incoming items! Most people never take the time required for clarifying into consideration. Our natural tendency is to stay active, and it is easy not to take the focused time to clarify all of the new "In." This results in having a backlog of unclarified items and being overwhelmed. Setting aside time each day to clarify your incoming is the only way to avoid becoming overwhelmed. Get your "In" to empty every day or so. Similarly, when you are away at a conference, an off-site meeting, or on vacation, you need to expect that it will require one hour to get caught up for each day you are out of the office! As you handle your incoming and keep your calendar and lists current, you will build trust in your system.

Step 5. Identify and address your limiting criteria.

Have you noticed that as you move through your day, there are **limiting criteria** that constrain what you are able to work on? Knowing what they are and what you can do about them can help you focus on those actions that are doable in the here and now. There are four main limiting criteria:

1. Context—What you can do is often based on where you are right now. Context refers to where you are—in your office, in your car, at home, in an airport—and what tools you have at hand—such as your phone or computer. Depending on the context, you need to look only at the next actions on your list that you can actually do where you are and with the tools you have with you.

2. Time Available—How much time do you have available right now? What you can do right now is limited by how much time you have before you must do something else. Having a meeting in fifteen minutes would prevent doing many actions that require more time to even start. So you'll need to pick a next action that you can complete, or make progress on, in the time that you have available.

3. Energy Available—Your energy level fluctuates during the day. Choose a task that matches your energy level. It may seem unlikely that a book about external workflow and how to effectively handle information, emails, and paper coming into your world would venture into a discussion of your energy level. However, it is a real factor, and when making decisions about what to work on now, ignoring the issue of your current energy level will have consequences. We may be expected to always have high energy at work, but the reality is that our physical, mental, and creative energy goes up and down throughout the day. To be most productive, choose actions that match your available energy. You likely know when your energy is best in the day for being creative or tackling a big project. Likewise, when you notice your energy has waned, select next actions that are easier to complete, such as busywork or administrative chores or errands, to get you up and moving. Moreover, sometimes the most effective thing to do right now is to take a break to walk around the block.

4. Priority—Which action has the highest priority? We all want to know the answer. With all I have to get done, what should I work on *now*? Keep in mind this notion about priorities: you don't *set* priorities; you *have* them.

Up to this point in implementing GTD, you have accumulated a list of projects and multiple next actions that is critical to lay the groundwork for making trusted choices about what to do. Once you have that total inventory of your commitments at hand, you can then utilize the limiting criteria (context, time, and energy) in an effective way to navigate your life and work, moment to moment.

STOP HERE

> **Take a moment to evaluate
> the limiting criteria in your life, right now!**

1. **Context**—Where am I . . . now? What associated restrictions or limitations does this present?
2. **Time Available**—How much time do I have available . . . now?
3. **Energy Available**—What is my energy level . . . now? And what do I have the energy to take on right now?

LOW   MEDIUM   HIGH

4. **Priority**—What is the most important thing I can do right now with the time and energy I have available?

Frequently Asked Questions

Engaging: Choosing What to Do Right Now

Prioritizing sounds easier said than done. How do I know I'm making the right priority decisions?

Learn to trust that little voice that knows you better than you do, and knows what's better for you than you do.

Listing your top ten things you think you have to complete, in order, doesn't work. You'll have a different priority set at 8:00 p.m. from what you had at 10:30 this morning. Sometimes the most important thing for you to do will be to water your plants.

It's fine to focus on the top few things that you need to work on, if nothing else changes for your day. Just don't get too invested in that list and feel frustrated when ad hoc tasks show up and change your focus.

Ralph Waldo Emerson said, "Trust thyself: every heart vibrates to that iron string."

How do I know when it's okay for me to take a break?

Allow yourself some buffer time each day. You want to maintain your energy and a clear mind, so take a break when you need to. If you are hungry, get a snack. If you have been sitting too long, go for a stroll. If you just came out of a stressful meeting, do what you need to get your focus and energy back.

How can I keep on top of work and still enjoy vacation time?

There's nothing inherently good or bad about being involved with professional things on a vacation. It all depends on the many variables in your situation. Here are some basic tips to help you keep on top of work items and enjoy a stress-free vacation:

● Do your best before you start a vacation to catch up, clean up, and get proactive and current in your work-related agreements and commitments.

- Identify "Vacation" as a project as soon as it's on your radar and define and complete the action steps for your vacation as soon as you can.
- Always have a capture tool with you. You don't have to process your captures until you return, but capture the idea when it is fresh.
- Give support staff your contact information and clarify ahead of time what might constitute an "emergency" when it would be appropriate to use it.
- Block out at least a full day or two on your calendar for catching up when you return.

Congratulations!
You have successfully completed Move 10!

Go to the last page of the Workbook and update
Your Progress Tracker with today's date!

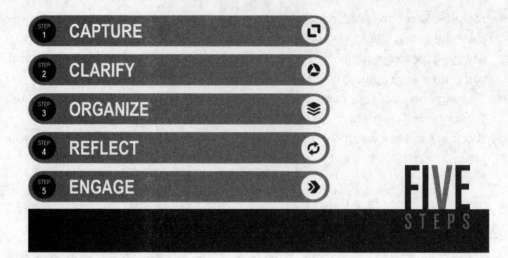

Your Engaging Checklist

Here are the recommended activities for deciding what to work on:

- ☐ I will conduct a daily review each morning or night before by checking my calendar and Next Actions lists.
- ☐ I will allow time for Clarifying and Organizing my incoming items (typically sixty to ninety minutes a day).
- ☐ I will use the four limiting criteria to make choosing "what to do now" easier: Context, Time Available, Energy Available, and Priority.

Congratulations!

You have just completed all 10 moves
to stress-free productivity!

Schedule time on your calendar to celebrate, or
if your celebration will take less than two minutes, do it now!

A (short but extremely helpful) Self-Assessment of Your Current Reality

DATE: _____

Now that you've gone through all ten moves, let's see how much your productivity has improved. Rate each of the following statements using the scale provided:

Rating Scale

1 = strongly disagree; **2** = disagree; **3** = neither agree nor disagree; **4** = agree; **5** = strongly agree

1	I write down ideas and to-do items when they first show up.	1	2	3	4	5
2	I keep a complete list of all my next actions.	1	2	3	4	5
3	I keep a record of what I am waiting for from other people.	1	2	3	4	5
4	My calendar contains only appointments or day-specific information that I need.	1	2	3	4	5
5	I have a single list of all my current projects.	1	2	3	4	5
6	I have at least one recorded next action for each of my projects.	1	2	3	4	5
7	I get my email inbox to zero every day or so by going through each email and putting it where it belongs.	1	2	3	4	5
8	I can store and access reference material easily when needed, whether it is paper or digital.	1	2	3	4	5
9	I have designated in-trays in all the places I need to capture all my incoming paper and stuff.	1	2	3	4	5

10	I get my paper in-tray(s) to empty every day or so.	1 2 3 4 5
11	When I get behind or overwhelmed, I know how to get back on track by engaging with my next actions, projects, and calendar.	1 2 3 4 5
12	I take time each week to get caught up and to review how I am doing with my professional/personal work.	1 2 3 4 5
13	I have a trusted place I can easily find and look at to see additional/support information about any project I am working on.	1 2 3 4 5
14	I have a framework I can use in order to best choose what to work on at any particular time.	1 2 3 4 5
15	When unexpected demands arise or interruptions occur, I can easily evaluate their priorities against everything else I have to do.	1 2 3 4 5

Total your score = _____ (out of 75)

Scoring Key

15–30: You really need this Workbook; don't worry, we will walk you through it.

31–46: You are getting a glimpse of what it feels like to live a productive life.

47–62: You are doing well! Keep going!

63–75: You are close to being masterful with GTD! This last fine-tuning will make a huge impact for you.

4

MORE

GTD STUFF

Bonus Insights and Practices

go.gettingthingsdone.com/no-12

Horizons of Focus®

go.gettingthingsdone.com/no-13

Resolving Paper Backlog

go.gettingthingsdone.com/no-14

Resolving Email Backlog

go.gettingthingsdone.com/no-15

Launching Projects with the Natural Planning Model®

go.gettingthingsdone.com/no-16

Getting Back on Track

Pursuing GTD Mastery

You likely have many areas of your life where there isn't necessarily an end point or a time when you have "arrived." For example, there is no end point to getting better, learning new habits, leading others, being fit, parenting, eating healthy, playing a musical instrument, practicing yoga or a martial art, or meditation or mindfulness.

As you continue your journey toward GTD mastery, you will gain greater long-term benefits in your work and in your life. Integrating the GTD moves into your life—for the *rest* of your life—will keep you on your path of GTD mastery. This requires continued focus, and you will see the benefits of GTD increase over time.

Just because you have completed the moves in this Workbook does not mean the journey of *learning* GTD is over. That would be like reading a book about fitness and then doing nothing about it. The same applies to building and maintaining the GTD system you've read about and started to apply in this Workbook—you have to keep being engaged with it. Here are some resources and ways to do so:

Books About GTD

David Allen's other books provide a deeper dive into GTD.

Getting Things Done

for Teens

take control of your life
in a distracting world

David Allen
NEW YORK TIMES bestselling author

Mike Williams and **Mark Wallace**

GettingThingsDone.com

Visit www.gettingthingsdone.com for:

- Schedule of upcoming public events
  - *Offered in the United States by our partner Vital Smarts, www.vitalsmarts.com*
  - *Offered around the world by our global partners, https://gettingthingsdone.com/ global-partners*
- Coaching services—GTD Focus in the United States and Canada, and our global partners in other regions, www.gtdfocus.com/services
- GTD Connect, the social community with resources such as videos and tools from certified GTD Trainers and Coaches
- The GTD blog at http://gettingthingsdone.com/gtd-times

GTD Connect

GTD Connect (www.GTDConnect.com) is a membership-based resource center for those who want to develop their GTD practice. Watch, listen, and learn on the GTD Connect site, download content to take with you on the go, and have it sent to you through the members-only distribution.

Members have unlimited access to:

- Webinars with David Allen and certified GTD Coaches on a wide range of productivity topics
- Extensive audio, video, and document libraries, including free downloads of the GTD Setup Guides for use with common software
- *Slice of GTD Life* series to see how others are making GTD stick
- David Allen's *In Conversation* interviews and the *Up Close with David* series
- Members-only discussion forums sharing ideas, tips, and tricks
- Hundreds of audio and video clips with David Allen and the certified GTD Coaches sharing tips and tricks

GTD Podcasts

Podcast episodes are available through:

- iTunes (https://itunes.apple.com/us/podcast/getting-things-done/id999098861)
- Stitcher (www.stitcher.com/podcast/getting-things-done)
- Libsyn (http://gettingthingsdone.libsyn.com)
- Google Play Music (https://play.google.com/music/listen#/ps/If5n66lnvvompn4q7yqu4cqxax4)
- Spotify (https://open.spotify.com/show/21mSaFgOhfR7TT8MKxF41n)

Your Path Forward

Congratulations on successfully completing *The Getting Things Done Workbook*. I hope this Workbook has been useful to you and that you are benefiting from getting more done with less effort and stress. You may discover, as others have, that there is more to the GTD methodology than meets the eye. Of particular note is the life-changing point of view that any problem can be seen as a project.

I really hope you have tasted the freedom of Mind Like Water and that your creative energies will be released by using these techniques. Be open to your own spirit, take appropriate risks, pay attention to the results, and course-correct as you move along your own unique Path of GTD Mastery.

Have a great rest of your life!

—*David Allen and Brandon Hall*

YOUR
PROGRESS

5

TRACKER

CAPTURE

Move 1	Capture All Your Incoming Paper into One In-tray	DATE
Move 2	Choose Your Capture Tool	DATE
Move 3	Do a Mind Sweep	DATE

CLARIFY

Move 4	Get Your In-Tray to Empty	DATE
Move 5	Get Your Emails to Zero	DATE

ORGANIZE

Move 6	Create Your Next Actions and Other Lists	DATE
Move 7	Keep Track of Your Projects on One List	DATE
Move 8	Create Folders to Stay Organized	DATE

REFLECT & ENGAGE

Move 9	Do a GTD Weekly Review	DATE
Move 10	Conduct a Daily Review	DATE

ACKNOWLEDGMENTS

We have deep gratitude for Treion Muller's many hours of expert help he gave to us in the design, tone, and developmental editing of the workbook.

Thanks to Mindy Powell for her assistance in developing its "moves."

We continue to appreciate our editor at Penguin Random House, Rick Kot, who gave us plenty of support through the project; and our agent, Doe Coover, who was key to triggering it.

Brandon particularly thanks Marian Bateman for her amazing coaching of him about GTD over many years. And this could not have come together without Kathryn Allen's tireless efforts in coordinating the moving parts.